The Christmas Miracle

THE
CHRISTMAS
Miracle

Experience the Blessing
JACK HAYFORD

Regal

A Division of Gospel Light
Ventura, California, U.S.A.

Published by Regal Books
A Division of Gospel Light
Ventura, California, U.S.A.
Printed in U.S.A.

Cover Design by Kevin Keller

Library of Congress Cataloging-in-Publication Data
Hayford, Jack W.
    The Christmas miracle / Jack Hayford.
       p.   cm.
    ISBN 0-8307-2507-5 (trade)
    ISBN 0-8307-2518-0 (hardcover)
    1. Christian life. 2. Conception—Religious aspects—Christianity.
    3. Mary, Blessed Virgin, Saint—Annunciation. I. Title.
    BV4501.2.H36873   1999   99-31667
    232.91—dc21   CIP

1 2 3 4 5 6 7 8 9 10 11 12 13 14 15 / 05 04 03 02 01 00 99

Rights for publishing this book in other languages are contracted by Gospel Literature International (GLINT). GLINT also provides technical help for the adaptation, translation and publishing of Bible study resources and books in scores of languages worldwide. For further information, write to GLINT at P.O. Box 4060, Ontario, CA 91761-1003, U.S.A. You may also send e-mail to Glintint@aol.com, or visit their web site at www.glint.org.

CONTENTS

PREFACE
9

INTRODUCTION
11

Part 1

THE IDEA OF INCARNATION

Part 2

THE MAID AND THE MIRACLE

Part 3

THE WAY MIRACLES HAPPEN

Part 4

LEARNING TO GROW WITH A MIRACLE

Preface

And Mary said:
"My soul magnifies the Lord,
And my spirit has rejoiced in God my
    Savior.
For He has regarded the lowly state of
    His maidservant;
For behold, henceforth all generations
    will call me blessed.
For He who is mighty has done great
    things for me,
And holy is His name.
And His mercy is on those who fear Him
From generation to generation.
He has shown strength with His arm;

He has scattered the proud in the
  imagination of their hearts.
He has put down the mighty from their
  thrones,
And exalted the lowly.
He has filled the hungry with good
  things,
And the rich He has sent away empty.
He has helped His servant Israel,
In remembrance of His mercy,
As He spoke to our fathers,
To Abraham and to his seed forever"
(Luke 1:46-55).

Introduction

The words "I'm pregnant" never fail to attract attention.

As a husband and a father, I've heard them spoken many times—four by my wife and (to date) a total of eight times by our kids, as grandchildren have been added to our family. The times we heard those words were all happy times.

But sometimes "I'm pregnant" is spoken in other ways:

- In fear, due to uncertainties, all the way from a mother's time of life to the question of a family's financial adequacy;
- In anger, because the relationship occasioning the pregnancy is insecure and the

likelihood of becoming abandoned and having to face everything alone is inflaming and embittering.

From joy to guilt, or from "Happy-to-be" to "What-will-happen-to-me?" the full spectrum of emotions surrounds the subject of pregnancy.

A pregnancy is the ultimate analogy. Everything in life is "like" it. As with a pregnancy, everything in life starts with a possibility and proceeds to a reality. The pattern of conception-to-delivery is rooted in the founding fundamentals of God's operational order of things. And life always is a miracle.

That's why I've written this little book. Because I want to point the way to life at its deepest, fullest and richest—at its miracle level.

To see life's miracle possibilities most clearly, I'm pointing to the most incredible and important pregnancy in history: Mary's. But don't make the mistake of thinking this is a book only for women or about babies.

This is a book for all genders, in its practicality.

It's a book for believers, prophetically.

And very much a book for you, personally.

I'm inviting you to travel with me to the drab, uninviting town called Nazareth, and to review how God is able to bring life into the most barren settings, and to breathe hope into the most unpromising situations.

The story we examine is too well known. It's been read so many Christmases that the seeds of wonder it holds have fallen on ears that hear only the one miracle: *His* birth. But the larger truth is that He, in fact, came to birth miracles in all of us as a way of life.

So come with me to the hills of Galilee; it's not a long climb. And I think you may find that your view of tomorrow may change from there.

Expectantly,
Jack Hayford
The Church On The Way
Van Nuys, California

PART 1

The Idea
of
Incarnation

NOW IN THE SIXTH MONTH THE ANGEL GABRIEL

WAS SENT BY GOD TO A CITY OF GALILEE NAMED

NAZARETH, TO A VIRGIN BETROTHED TO A MAN

WHOSE NAME WAS JOSEPH, OF THE HOUSE OF DAVID.

THE VIRGIN'S NAME WAS MARY. —LUKE 1:26,27

It may seem stark, but incarnation has to do with people "getting pregnant," expecting more than they ever dreamed, becoming open to possibilities they could never realize by themselves.

CHAPTER ONE

A Timeless Kind of Wonder

It started when Phil became pregnant. That's probably the moment God began to bring greatness out of the garbage.

Ted's pregnancy came full term when he decided to deal with the abortion he had financed in college for the coed he had been with.

Mine began in a car on the freeway—and God spoke.

Still a Miracle Worker Today

The words in the opening paragraphs contain no mistakes. Don't let the gender references throw you. "Three men? Pregnant?" But that's what happens when the "Mary miracle" touches any person. It's just as likely to happen to a man as a woman, just as I learned more than twenty Christmases ago. Heaven is still waiting to pour promise into earth's most unlikely places.

The God who chose a virgin girl as the avenue through whom He would miraculously give mankind His greatest gift is still working that "Mary" kind of miracle today. That is to say: What the Almighty did then in the physical/biological realm—supernaturally begetting life, promise and hope where none existed—He is fully ready and able to do now in virtually any realm.

He does this same kind of thing today—in marriages, in businesses, in hearts, minds and souls. Where life or love, hope or strength, promise or patience have disappeared—or never been present at all—He comes to offer the Mary miracle. It's a timeless kind of wonder that is still being worked by our changeless heavenly Father.

It isn't mystical, though it is miraculous. That's probably the hardest part to explain because our human disposition is to turn God's imminent availability to us into a distant improbability. Most people I meet believe He's there some-where, but hardly here—now—for them. Too many think the Mary miracle is only for the "Saint Marys," and reasoning men and women tend to conclude that even if there is more than one Saint Mary, "I certainly don't qualify!"

"Me? A candidate for a visit from God? The Almighty offering me the promise of things I feel are totally outside the scope of probability if not possibility?"

But I'm writing to that very kind of person—the thinker who wonders if God is that direct, personal or ready to visit them. And the answer is yes—to you! In spite of our finiteness, our fallibility and our fears, you and I are candidates for such a visitation because qualifying for the Mary miracle doesn't require a self-accomplished goodness. It only calls us to be open to a God-appointed grace.

The Mary miracle calls us all to come back to a moment when eternity penetrated time with the power that can change all our days and hours, our lives—past, present and future. That incredible encounter—when a Jewish maiden named Mary was met with divine grace in a dusty town called Nazareth two thousand years ago—set forward more than the incarnation of the world's Savior.

Mary's miracle opens the promise—indeed, the pathway—for God to incarnate His gracious purpose and power in the experience of anyone who will open to the same order of miracle. Because God is no respecter of persons,[1] He shows what He can do in some lives, as a sample of what He can do in all lives. He does these apparently "occasional wonders," not to preempt our hopes for the same, but to promote them. So in Mary He brought to reality the ultimate hope—Jesus—and in doing that He pointed not only to the way of salvation, but also to the possibilities of "Christ in *you*, the hope of glory."[2]

That "order of miracle"—that genre, dimension or type called the "Mary miracle"—is not solely defined by the astounding *physical* reality of the supernatural conception Mary experienced. Because even then the miracle wasn't *only* physical. Beyond that biologically transcendent event, when a real child was generated within a virgin womb by the creative power of God's declared Word, heaven came down to us.

Heaven came to touch your world and mine, as well as Mary's. Not only in the broad and sweeping ways we usually concede when we appropriately affirm the beauty of the fact: "For God so loved the world that He gave His only begotten Son, that whoever believes in Him should not perish but have everlasting life."[3] But with and beyond so great salvation, in the most intimate and personal ways, the Mary miracle holds the promised potential of heaven's entry into all our life circumstances—yours and mine.

I want to press this precious point: The Mary miracle was never intended to be only Mary's! Just as surely as the Savior she bore is for each of us to receive personally, so is the type of miracle she experienced. The Mary miracle contains a pattern for possibilities, a template of truth: Miracles are intended to happen within, through and around you and me, too!

Being Open to God's Unlimited Possibilities

I am deeply committed to helping people to be open, as Mary was, to God's divine possibilities for their personal lives. This means we need to be open to God's miracle grace and power; to the way He calls us all to break through the intellectual membrane that tends to separate our minds from our hearts. The Holy Spirit wants to press into the innermost sanctuary of our lives, where daily realities brutally frame situations that either disintegrate our dreams or incarcerate our hopes.

Those difficult, tough or problematic things that invade homes, work, family, minds and habit have a way of taking over, of dictating restricted dimensions. Too readily we submit to them, supposing "this is how I guess it's intended to be."

But the Holy Spirit is ready to bring us through and beyond those "controlling or limiting circumstances," as we call them.

What are yours?

Every honest person knows they are there.

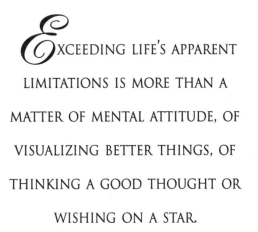

Exceeding life's apparent limitations is more than a matter of mental attitude, of visualizing better things, of thinking a good thought or wishing on a star.

Life unaided by divine grace does have limits, but they are by no means all ordained by God, whose unlimited power invites us beyond life's limits. However, He—the Living God—is essential to our transcending such limits, difficulties or barricades. Exceeding life's apparent limitations is more than a matter of mental attitude, of visualizing better things, of thinking a good thought or wishing on a star.

Mary's miracle was neither spawned by human seed nor generated by a mystic style of meditation. She had neither sexual intercourse nor an intellectual enlightenment because the Mary miracle is neither physical nor mental in its source. It is from God, the Creator of all, coming to us individually to say, "I'm not finished creating yet."

God said that to me on the freeway.

❧

CHAPTER TWO

A Voice You Can Trust

It was a month past Christmas as I drove out to the San Fernando Valley, en route from the college where I was teaching to the small church I had just begun pastoring part-time.

The hum of my car's engine almost harmonized with the buzz of cars zipping past, as drivers capitalized on the early afternoon's yet-unclogged condition of the Los Angeles freeway system. I didn't know it, but I was about to have a visitation—a kind of "meeting with God." I'm persuaded most people experience these at different times and in different ways, but are afraid to tell anyone, or even afraid to admit it to themselves. But I'm going to tell of my experiencing such a meeting.

A Divine Visitation on the Freeway

I was fully awake, entirely coherent, and totally unprepared and unexpectant—not even slightly prone to seeking a mystical encounter. Even if I was, I certainly would not have been searching for it on a Los Angeles freeway! But I had just angled to flow with traffic onto the Hollywood Freeway, and I was noting the slight but remaining glory of the leaves still clustered on the trees to my right.

North Hollywood's Chandler Park is split by the highway at that point, and though Southern California's winter is genuinely chilly and some rains had already come, this afternoon's pale January sun still brought a remembrance of autumn to the scene. I changed lanes to move around an older car chugging along in its vain attempt to keep pace with the traffic, when it happened.

You mustn't think too small.

Someone else had spoken. It wasn't me, and no one else was in the car, at least no one I could see.

You mustn't think too small, or you'll get in My way.

I knew the Voice, but was completely unready for the words. And I was without the slightest notion of what was about to be said.

I've set Myself to do a great work.

Nothing had changed, except everything. In less than 30 seconds, I had been snatched from my mundane thought processes, occupied only with navigating my car, into a sudden sense of The Presence. God was here, talking to me. I knew I was hearing a Voice I could trust. I had learned to hear Him over years of walking with Him, and without labored, analytical reasoning, I intuitively and instantly knew why He was saying these words.

Although God's voice may surprise us at times, when it's truly Him speaking, He usually makes clear what He's talking about. Even when we don't yet understand all the significance within His words or promise, we can grasp the general intent of His prompting and tune in. So that day I knew why I needed jarring from the smallness of my own vision. Still, I had no idea of the scope of what God meant, only that He was arresting my attention, inviting my openness to His mightiness.

The staggering possibilities His words "great work" portended, I would only begin to understand over the years to come, but my immediate problem was to know how to respond to the stunning reality of that moment of direct confrontation: What's this? Who am I to receive such a word of promise?

I said as much, whispering my heart's bewilderment. "Lord, why should I be part of something great You would do?" His answer brought tears to my eyes, as I was reminded of the vastness of God's grace that flows to those who acknowledge their helplessness and let Him into their lives. He reminded me that my very life is a miracle, as is all of ours.

I have told more about the fruit of that encounter, writing elsewhere of the amazing things the Lord has done since that day. But I make this much mention here because it was an "impregnating moment"—that order of visit from God that sets the Mary "kind" of miracle in motion. It was an unplanned-for encounter in which the Creator gave notice of His desire to open my life to His purposes that He might flow His promise through me.

Identifying God's Voice

God does these things with people. People like you. For if anything is clear to me about that particular moment (besides the fact that God was seeking to get my attention), it is that my moment was unique only in that it was mine. I knew then, and I know now, that such moments are given to every human being—sometime. They're the moments the potential of the Mary miracle is introduced to us as an awakening—as a call to permit hope, to allow *expectation* into our hearts.

I want to help people identify and accept this fact, and to become unafraid to acknowledge and respond to it. I'm convinced it not only has already occurred in some way with most people, but also that it will, if it hasn't yet. And even before I invite you to trace the details with me as we look at Mary's moment in the record of the Holy Scriptures, I want to define what I mean by God's "speaking" to you. I want you to be clear that I'm not peddling some form of self-hypnosis or subjective psychological gamesmanship.

It's important to know the difference between meeting God and muddling with goofiness. I always want to sidestep silliness, avoid deception, refuse mysticism, overcome fear and deny self-importance. All five of these deceivers, the threats of which intimidate so many people from acknowledging God's "voice" to them, can and should be dismissed if we're to wisely open ourselves to the Mary miracle. God's is a voice you can trust, and when He speaks none of the following are present.

• Silly Notions

Silly notions proposed by crackpots, or even sincere-but-unwise saints, should be easy to dispense with. And they should be the quickest for us to sidestep as well because God is never goony nor graceless.

God isn't going to say, "Hi there! I think I'll do something great, so quit your job, leave your wife, abandon your kids and go to Indonesia next Thursday!" He *will* call us to faith and to action, but not without sensible regard for others and not without reasonable processes of time and providential circumstances marking the way.

• Deception

Deception is not difficult to avoid. Any "word" that doesn't align with God's Word in the Holy Scriptures not only can be dismissed at once, but must be. When the Lord said to me, "I've set Myself to do a great work," it not only *sounded* like God's way of speaking, but the Bible *resounds* with such promises: "Be strong and very courageous [bold] for the Lord your God is with you."[1]

Our only need is to remember three things: If God's voice to me is true, (1) I don't need to announce it to others; (2) I'm not required to prove it by loveless words or deeds; and (3) it isn't mine to fulfill. If it's God, He'll bring it about as I wait on Him—Him alone!

- Mysticism

Mysticism is the idea that only a select breed of pensive, reclusive, religiously inclined souls ever hear the voice of God. But everything in the Bible argues to the contrary.

Working men and busy women are the subjects of His will, the objects of His creative purposes and the recipients of holy promptings from Him. Jesus spoke to fishermen working to earn a living, accountants who needed to balance books to meet legal specifications and political activists concerned with social justice. God spoke to Mary as a workaday woman, Sarah as a housewife and Esther as a surprised-to-have-made-it-here queen. These were the kinds of men and women He called then, and the Lord speaks to such commonplace people today. You're not out of His "broadcast range."

Tuning in to the Holy Spirit's voice and moving to a monastery are two completely different things. You don't have to do the second to realize the first. God likes to talk to everyday people, and He does—every day.

- Fear

Fear is perhaps the most challenging obstacle to our opening to God's voice and believing Him. On the one hand is our fear of the cost of commitment, and on the other the fear of failure.

We often fear faith will cost too much or that we'll do too little. But God's call is not a threat; it's the promise of a possibility. He speaks to let us know what He can do if we'll allow Him. God's words, spoken in the secret places of our souls, are an invitation love makes to receive His actions, not a heavenly dictum demanding our achievement.

He calls us all to greater possibilities than we could ever produce ourselves, asking only that we let Him work with and through us. We can begin by permitting love's invitation to drive out fear's inhibitions.[2]

- Self-Importance

"But," some ask, "might I think too much of myself if God does speak, and then does do something wonderful in my life? I wouldn't want to give place to pride."

Oh, dear friend, how many submit to this supposedly humble proposition! But I want to urge you to be at peace, because God's gracious workings in your life will never confuse you about who the "great one" is if you keep focused on Him. He'll keep our perspective clear, and only a fool will be duped by delusions of self-grandeur.

For example, it is one thing that God said to me, "I've set Myself to do a great work." But it would have been quite another if I claimed He had said, "I'm going to make you the greatest person in history"; or, "Nothing I've ever done in the world will match the great thing I'm going to do through you."

God's call for us to believe He has

God's voice is not difficult to distinguish from the pitifully confusing sounds of man's silly sayings, or from the frighteningly erroneous subtleties of the serpent's hissings.

❧

wonder-workings in store for us—our own order of "Mary miracles"—focuses on *His* greatness, not ours. To say yes to the Lord's high promises for your life will never indulge pride. Why? Because once

He begins doing what He promises, you'll be so amazed you'll only be able to praise Him, and to point the path for others to do the same.

Yes, child of the Father, you can trust His voice. It's not difficult to distinguish from the pitifully confusing sounds of humankind's silly sayings, or from the frighteningly erroneous subtleties of the serpent's hissings.

There's a purity and clarity in the Holy Spirit's call to you when He says, "Come back to the fountainhead miracle, so you can learn to flow in the stream of the Father's present wonder-workings intended for you."

❧

CHAPTER THREE

The Fountainhead Miracle

The Mary miracle is the fountainhead miracle; it's the beginning of all God's wonder-works of redemption.

Redemption is the beautiful word that embraces all of God's divine program of recovery: His reclaiming the lost, forgiving the sinful and then setting about to fulfill His purposes in each one who will receive His offer of love and life. That's what redemption is about.

It didn't start in a manger in Bethlehem, but in a womb in Nazareth. Even more precisely, it began before all time in the mind of the eternal

Father. From the fountainhead of God's redeeming grace, the Mary miracle flowed from heaven to earth, from out of eternity into time. And here, within time, that miracle began to take shape in a Galilean girl who was stunned by the wonder of what had come to her. That summarizes the way the Mary miracle begins in, and flows forward with, anyone.

The Mary miracle starts with the living God ready to work something of His releasing grace, and continues with His finding someone willing to become an instrument of that grace. It is best understood by looking closely at that incredible starting point of all redemption's miracles: the Incarnation.

What happened in the willingness of God to accept temporary housing in a womb, in order to bring eternal promise into the world, is, of course, the theme of Christmas. But it is the source of every other holy day as well, for no other date on the calendar of our holy celebrations would exist without the beginning—the birth. There are no miracles without the Mary miracle.

Furthermore, the story of the glory revealed in Jesus Christ our Savior has another incredible feature. In addition to God's willingness to come to us is the overarching phenomenon of His coming through a human conduit. The Mary miracle reminds us that God Himself has chosen no beginning point for His wonder-workings apart from human beings. In Mary, He demonstrated His readiness and willingness to work through an imperfect human vessel, and He is still unashamed to do the same.

Capture this truth, dear one.

As amazing as is God's will to come from heaven to earth, an even more transcending grace is manifest in His choice to reveal Himself through the fabric and frame of humankind. Look what happened to Mary.

Here was a common member of Adam's race as tainted by the Fall as any other. But she was chosen. And an equal splendor is the revelation God's Word gives to us that we are no less His choice: "Just as He chose us in Him before the foundation of the world."[1]

Mary was the first person to experience this order of being chosen, of becoming a vehicle of redemption's fullest and highest expression of grace. Consider this:

God's redemptive promise was brought *to* her, to grow *in* her, to be delivered *through* her, to change the world *around* her. Read it again, and aloud. Say it over another time, because in these words we're learning the essence of the Mary miracle. However, before we further our study of how her miracle forecasts yours and mine, let's relish the unique wonder at this fountain-head.

The promise was:

- brought *to* her: the angel's announcement;
- to grow *in* her: the miraculous conception;
- to be delivered *through* her: that first Christmas;
- to change the world *around* her: through Calvary's triumph.

The promise was the ultimate Word — the pre-existent Logos, the eternal second Person of the Godhead called the Son — becoming a man, incarnate through the Mary miracle. He was named Jesus, and since then both heaven and earth worship Him as the worthy redeemer.

- The Lamb was born in a manger to be sacrificed on a cross.
- The only begotten Son of the highest was conceived and born to spend His life as the price to regain a lost race.

"Pleased as man with men to dwell, Jesus, our Emmanuel."[2]

It Starts with the Mary Miracle

God came down, became one of us, came to walk with us, finally to die for us. And as the trail of miracles He leaves stretches from Cana in Galilee to Jerusalem in Judea, its fountainhead is found in Nazareth. The Mary miracle starts it all. This is crucially important to see.

To see that miracle for all its worth is to do more than give appropriate and humble gratitude for the fact that God *came* to us, becoming incarnate as a man—a *transcendent wonder!*

To see the implications of the Mary miracle is to do more than receive the Savior; yielding to faith in Jesus as both—the miracle-working Master and the dying-to-rise-again Savior—a *redeeming wonder!*

But please distinguish these wonders from yet another. Because to see the Mary miracle clearly is not only to receive and believe the gift we have been given through the miracle of Christ's incarnation and work of salvation. It is also to see the way God works redemptively—it is to grasp the *continuing wonder!*

God's choice to use Mary, a mere human vessel through which to unfold His wonder-working toward mankind, discloses an incredible fact. God thereby revealed His willingness to bring

His promises to nest in fallen human vessels. If they will open to such grace, He is ready to change their world—*through them!* To see and grasp this is to pave the way for the Mary miracle to occur over and over again.

Not in the biological sense.

WE MUSTN'T MINIMIZE THE PROMISE, THE HOPE, THAT MARY'S MIRACLE AFFORDS US BECAUSE THE FATHER IS STILL LOOKING FOR HUMAN VESSELS THROUGH WHOM HE CAN FURTHER HIS REDEMPTIVE PURPOSES.

Not in the "only-begotten" sense.

But it is to see how God, through His promise of life in Jesus Christ, is still seeking to bring His promise *to*, *in* and *through* us, to change things *around* us.

There is a triple wonder in the idea of the Incarnation: (1) a transcendent wonder in the Creator stooping to become a creature; (2) a redemptive wonder in the sinless Savior surrendering to die for a rebel race; and then one more, (3) a continuing wonder.

It's the wonder that all this not only provides you and me with a way to receive forgiveness and eternal life, but also that the process of God's "incarnation idea" continues right up to this moment. He who used Mary to introduce the Redeemer is ready to continually work the wonders of redemption's power through people today—to people like us.

The Mary miracle opened a river of revealed grace: God is pleased to use humans—wonderfully! To emphasize that wonder is not to minimize the uniqueness of the wonder Mary delivered. Jesus is *the* Redeemer and, as such, is the Most Wonderful. But neither let us minimize the promise, the hope, that Mary's miracle affords us because the Father is still looking for human vessels through whom He can further His redemptive purposes.

The fountainhead miracle is the Mary miracle, because the fount of redemption—Jesus

Himself—came to us through that wonder. But the river is still flowing, and God's Spirit is calling us all to move into the stream.

There are promises He wants to bring *to* you, (concerning arenas of need, hope or longing you are aware of, where God's power and grace are needed);

...which promises He wants to grow *in* you, (as you receive His Word and entertain the possibility that there is nothing too hard for God);

...that He may work His promised wonders *through* you, (as a humble vessel, submitted to His grace and dependent upon His sufficiency and power);

...in order to change the world *around* you (be it your family, your relationships, your neighborhood, city or nation, your church or your circumstance).

And all this takes time...sometimes more than we would like. But, then, it took Mary nine months.

Or was it thirty years?

❧

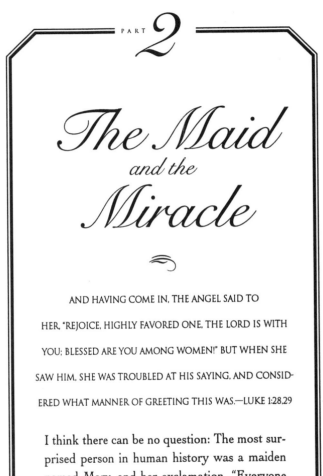

PART 2

The Maid
and the
Miracle

AND HAVING COME IN, THE ANGEL SAID TO
HER, "REJOICE, HIGHLY FAVORED ONE, THE LORD IS WITH
YOU; BLESSED ARE YOU AMONG WOMEN!" BUT WHEN SHE
SAW HIM, SHE WAS TROUBLED AT HIS SAYING, AND CONSID-
ERED WHAT MANNER OF GREETING THIS WAS.—LUKE 1:28,29

I think there can be no question: The most surprised person in human history was a maiden
named Mary, and her exclamation, "Everyone
will call me blessed," was a declaration of surprise, not a claim to adulation.

CHAPTER FOUR

Try to Picture Ordinariness

What kind of day was it in Nazareth? And what was Mary doing when the angel appeared? Try to picture ordinariness instead of splendor or mystic radiance. A rainy day instead of sunshine. Winter instead of springtime.

Most of our poetic notions need to be challenged if we're to be open to the Mary miracle. Why? Because if we clothe the original in lavish garments of imagined unnaturalness, we'll suppose that supernatural happenings only come to superb settings. But God clothes Himself in the ordinary, coming to ordinary people, and He is no less able to do the extraordinary for having come to the world's Nazareths.

It ought to be easy to shake off dreamy-eyed ideas about the setting of the Incarnation. Years later, a blunt-tongued disciple-to-be would hear of Jesus' hometown origins and say, "Nazareth! What good can come from there?"[1] And because God chose a most unlikely town to introduce the Mary miracle, we can probably count on everything else being improbable, too.

God Doesn't Need a Setting

I was charmed by a magnificent staging I saw years ago, dramatically re-creating the angel's announcement to Mary. She was singing in a garden, gorgeously attired in a pure white dress and sky-blue shawl. Birdsong filled the air, flowers bloomed in profusion and ivy dripped over the walls, providing an inviting scene that undoubtedly answered something akin to each viewer's fairy-tale kind of supposition of exactly how it ought to have been. But Mary's story isn't a fairy tale!

And because God refused to give His Son a silver-spoon-in-the-mouth entrance into the world, there's no reason for us to invent magnificence. It's enough to have an astonishing promise offered and a miraculous conception occur. God doesn't need a contrived setting to get Him into the mood for miracles. He simply sends His word of promise to ordinary people living in the most ordinary situations.

Let's ask some unanswerable questions:

- Was Mary at prayer when the annunciation occurred, or perhaps washing dishes? Or scrubbing clothes?
- Was there a shaft of light upon her countenance, or a streak of perspiration?
- Was she at a quiet, convenient time in her day, or was this encounter an interruption?
- Was she poised, as though having read a script in advance, or just plain frightened by the angel's sudden appearance?

Let's keep asking:

- Had Mary's parents taught her to believe "you could be the one"? Or had such a thought never occurred in her wildest imaginations?
- Was her family financially fixed, or was Mary's betrothal to Joseph an economic relief for their strained budget?

- Was she beautiful, socially adept and personally desirable? Or was Mary possibly only a plain girl with a simple faith, raised in an ordinary home, scheduled for an arranged marriage and headed for a predictably uneventful future married to the town carpenter?

The Story Doesn't Require Elegance

These questions aren't meant to mount a crusade against tradition, but to force us into a confrontation with truth. The truth is that nothing in the Bible requires elegance in this part of the story. In fact, the tone of the text argues for Mary's situation to have been among the lowliest. Listen to her sing several days later:

> For He has regarded the lowly state of His maidservant;...He has...exalted the lowly. He has filled the hungry (Luke 1:48,52,53).

These are not the words of a fictionalized Grimm's princess waiting to be discovered by her Prince Charming. Frankly, they sound more like the words of an ordinary, if not poor, girl, who has suddenly had the simplicity of her world invaded with majestic hope.

Let's get it right. This baby will be born in a barn and shortly have to escape under the point of a vicious king's sword, so we're outright presumptuous if we think anything is going to come easy. And later, in this same town, He'll be assailed by the hard-nosed thanklessness of skeptics dulled in faith by the wearying effect of the inane in their less-than-happy world. Yes, *do* get it right: Nazareth was no center of spiritual promise.

But the Promise came there.

And you and I are wise to take this to heart because it's a too often overlooked fact, and it's one of deep importance to us as we study the Mary miracle. There is an availability of almightiness—God's. It's waiting in the wings to come on stage where flies fill the air, where unpleasant smells annoy the senses and where end-of-the-line circumstances declare, "no hope."

Hannah, the prophet Samuel's mother, was another girl who was surprised by God's miracle grace in an unlikely setting. Her words seem to harmonize with Mary's:

> My heart rejoiceth in the Lord,...He raiseth up the poor out of the dust, and

lifteth up the beggar from the dunghill, to set them among princes (1 Sam. 2:1,8, *KJV*).

*O*UR LOVING GOD IS AS INTERESTED IN INCARNATING HIS HOPE AND PROMISE WHERE YOU LIVE—RIGHT NOW—AS HE WAS WHEN HE SENT THE FOUNTAIN-HEAD PROMISE TO NAZARETH TWENTY CENTURIES AGO.

❧

Hannah reminds us that *dunghills* (it can't get more graphic than that!) don't inhibit God's dealings or limit our destinies. But they often are God's starting place. And everything we can gather of popular opinion in Mary's day is that Nazareth was one.

So in that light, let none of us live without hope. Our loving God is as interested in incarnating His hope and promise where you live—right now—as He was when He sent the fountainhead promise to Nazareth twenty centuries ago. It's important that such a conviction become fixed in our souls. For only thereby will we find it fully credible, and thus embraceable, that the Father of all promise is willing to father His fullest promise in the ordinariness of our own personal setting—however unpleasant, however unlikely.

We Don't Have to be Sinless

And another thing: Concerning the girl from Nazareth, she was like you and me—she wasn't sinless either.

It's not comfortable for me to bluntly assert that because I respect the sincerity of those whose reverence for Mary is rooted in the proposition of her "immaculate conception." Those two words frame a tradition that suggest Mary was somehow born miraculously herself; somehow kept forever sinless from birth, in a way that prevented her having inherited any sin in her own nature or person.

To deny this, as we must, isn't to adopt an unkind spirit or to attack sensitive souls. As you'll see, I have nothing but the highest regard for this maid of Nazareth who became the mother of God. But in studying her accurately and biblically, I'm not required to scathe those who have created a structure of unnecessary tradition around her.

Still, to see Mary for all she does have to teach us, we must hold to the simple truth, distinguishing between it and some of tradition's unessential enhancements. Mary didn't need to be a sinless human to become the bearer of the sinless Savior, and she wasn't. I affirmed this because Mary herself, like every human being since the first pair, was of the fallen Adam's seed. But the blessed truth is that this constituted no hindrance, for the Creator-Father is able to beget His untainted-by-the-Fall Son within this woman's womb without the help of an invented doctrine. How He did it — fusing deity with humanity — is His to achieve wondrously and ours to accept worshipfully.

Uncluttered.

Unembellished.

Plain and simple. The same way all of God's salvation processes work — without human invention, and beyond human understanding.

Mary's humanness is essential to our fully appreciating her miracle. Only then can we see how determined God was to become incarnate as one of us, and to work a wonder to achieve it. But to see that wonder is also to see how committed

He is to work beyond our helplessness; to move in upon us with His ability to redeem our hopelessness as well. In Mary, the same One who spoke into the chaotic disorder of the Genesis "void," and brought light and life, spoke promise into the tainted humanness of her virgin womb and begot the Light of the world—bringing Life to all humankind.

Since that moment, the Light has kept increasing, and His Life has kept on multiplying in thousands of "wombs of circumstance" where other members of Adam's race open themselves—first to Mary's Son, and then to the patterns of possibility revealed in her miracle.

The Mary miracle first happened to an ordinary sinner in an ordinary town to set forth this lesson for all learners: Nothing is impossible where you live either—no matter who you are. Because salvation has come to save, this greatest of all miracles—once received—holds in it the seeds of any number of wonders.

The gift keeps on giving!

❦

CHAPTER FIVE

Amazed in the Presence

I think there can be no question: The most surprised person in human history has to be a girl named Mary. Stripped of religious pageantry's stiltedness, everything about her amazed response to the angel's shocking announcement shouts the fact that this young woman had no illusions about herself.

Where Does Mary Fit Today?

"What in the world are you saying?" she exclaims, doubtless gasping for breath as she asks, *"Me?"*

There's no reason to think she ever changed her unassuming air; no reason to suppose we're obligated to affect special honor toward her because neither God nor Mary ever suggested we do.

But we can certainly learn a lot from her.

Mary is a study in several wonderful features of a dynamic life of faith.

- First, she knows how to *respond* when God offers miracles (she welcomes His wonder-workings).
- Second, she knows how to *think* when people give her prophecies about her life (she doesn't push for the prophecies' fulfillment, but ponders them patiently, leaving them in God's hands).
- Third, she knows what to *say* when she doesn't understand what God is doing with her life ("Whatever He [Jesus] says to you, do it!")[1].
- Fourth, Mary knows how to *grow* when one stage of God's miracle-working in her life is ready to pass to another (see her in the Upper Room, waiting for the Spirit's empowering, right along with other disciples).

But perhaps the most important thing for us to

see is how all this started. We need to note the beginning of her walk into the miraculous, to see how she viewed her role in the amazing thing that was happening to her, and what was about to happen *in* and *through* her. To do this, we may find we have a lot of baggage to unload.

I really don't know how to account for either the fuss or the furor that has risen up around Mary. Whether it's the protests of people who object to her receiving any recognition at all, or the problem that some adulate or nearly deify her—both seem to miss the issue. Mary *did* become the mother of Jesus, and Mary *does* provide a model for studying how God's grace can fill every life with promise. She deserves special attention:

- She is the human avenue through which is introduced the miracle One bringing God's saving grace to humankind. We all need to learn that first. Then,
- She is the "first of a kind"; the prototype, if you will, of the way God works to bring His wonders unto and through people. And let's all learn of this, too.

Both of these features command our consideration: her delivery of the virgin-born Son of God our Savior, and her experience of God's way of working miraculously in and through those who are receptively open to Him.

Yes, Mary deserves our study of the place God has put her in the history of His dealings with humankind, but we can't make a practical, freeing application of the principles she illustrates without addressing the question: "Where does Mary 'fit' today?" Because whether she has been virtually banished from the thoughts of some, or unduly "blessed" by the considerations of others, we will profit in finding the biblical balance on the subject of her uniqueness. She was entirely unique in her role as the biological mother of our Lord, but God's Word also shows she was entirely the same as us in virtually every other way—as a subject of God's grace, as a person needing comfort and assurance, and as a worshiper amazed at God's greatness being shown to her. To see how she is called "blessed among women" can, I think, provide a freeing perspective on Mary's place in God's divine order.

Blessed Among Women

A form of these words occurs three times in the text of Luke's Gospel. They seem to be the hinge upon which misunderstanding turns and by which misapplication (or application at all) takes place. Strained meanings of the phrase "blessed are you among women"[2] cause many to separate camps. Some conclude in affording her no respect at all — rejecting any acknowledgment of her distinct and privileged role; others conclude they are duty bound to render unusual respect — reverencing her in a way untaught by God's Word. But to look at each instance in which these words are spoken — (1) by Gabriel, (2) by Elizabeth, and (3) by Mary herself — may be helpful to all of us.

Gabriel's Greeting

> And having come in, the angel said to her, "Rejoice, highly favored one, the Lord is with you; blessed are you among women!" (Luke 1:28).

First, clarity immediately comes to the use of the word "blessed" as used regarding Mary, when we begin by noting how Gabriel's words were focused on God's grace. They were extolling nothing of a particular worthiness on Mary's part, but declarative of the holy graciousness of The Highest. The word "blessed" *(eulogeo)* is a simple, forthright prophecy — "You are (and will be) *well spoken of.*" It's an assuring, affirming word, given to allay the fear inciting the shock such a sudden encounter would bring. Gabriel is handling the problem we usually find in the Scriptures when angels visit people; there's a need to cushion the moment, to soften the shocked surprise. It's as though the angel is saying, "You're not seeing an apparition or being solicited by a devil—the Lord is with you, and the intent of this moment is blessing. Be at peace."

But what most clearly indicates the idea in the phrase "blessed are you" is the statement that precedes it. "Rejoice, highly favored one," provides a context for our understanding. Because before Mary is told "You are blessed" (that is, "will be highly spoken of"), Gabriel had called her to rejoice—and for a reason: "You are highly favored!" That's good advice to a recipient of God's grace, not a promotion to a position of superiority.

The Greek verb expressing Gabriel's declaration of God's gracious generosity toward Mary is *charitoo*. It's derived from the root *charis*, "grace," and is expansive in its richness, properly allowing the translation, "highly favored." It literally conveys the idea of a person's being "uniquely privileged," that is, afforded a once-in-all-history role. *Charitoo* is employed significantly to describe Mary's case, as the privileged bearer of the Christ child. Hers was a "once-in-history" role, but the Word of God seems clearly intent on emphasizing this same "once-in-history" fact about every one of us. Astoundingly, precisely this same word used of Mary is used in the Bible of you and me. The ennobling verb *charitoo* is amazingly enough found in only two places: in Luke 1, of Mary, and in Ephesians 1 of each and every believer in Jesus Christ!

- Of Mary: *Charitoo* is used in Luke 1:28, and provides the explanation as to why she is called "blessed." As one "uniquely graced" she was given a unique role: No one else has been either called or privileged to serve the place she was given.
- Of each believer: *Charitoo* is used in Ephesians 1:6, and joined to the fact that each of us have been called "blessed" also (Eph. 1:3). As ones who are "chosen" (Eph. 1:4), we each have a unique role assigned to no one else than ourselves, individually.

It is an awesome, biblical fact that the Holy Spirit moved the apostle Paul to seize this same word, only used one other time in reference to the Virgin Mary, and apply it to every one of the

Lord's redeemed! That parallel use of this great word dramatically demonstrates the validity of our seeing the Mary miracle as an invitation to our expectancy toward something of the same.

MARY WAS UNIQUELY

PRIVILEGED—BUT SO ARE YOU.

GOD IS STILL SEEKING HUMAN

VESSELS WHO NEED GRACE, UNTO

AND THROUGH WHOM HE CAN

POUR GRACE, WORKING MIGHTILY

AND MAGNIFICENTLY.

We are *meant* to see the way her experience forecasts possibilities for our own!

Yes, Mary was uniquely privileged—but so are you, dear one. Because in that one word, "grace," we're taught that Mary's miracle was not given to her credit but unto her blessing. And the same applies to each of us, for God is still seeking human vessels who *need* grace, unto and through whom He can *pour* grace, working mightily and magnificently.

Further, please see how this truth breathes in the very first word the angel spoke to Mary— "Rejoice!" I mention this, not only because it's the logical beginning of praise that God's promised grace should evoke from us. But some older translations have Gabriel's greeting opening with the word, "Hail!" In centuries past, it was the right word because "hail" simply meant, "Be happy and healthy!" It was a greeting with hope and promise, not an elevation of a person above others. The angel used this word to say, "Something good is about to happen to you!" Both Gabriel and Mary were unconfused about what was happening: The Creator God was up to something almighty and wonderful. But it was wholly granted by His grace and to be entirely accomplished for His glory, even though she was the privileged participant—a happy victim of God's glorious grace.

So let us see it clearly: God's wonder-workings are all grace-workings. It's a fundamental necessity for us to grasp that truth because it inevitably will liberate us:

- Freeing us from mistaken notions about Mary;
- Freeing us from making celebrities of outstanding spiritual leaders;
- Freeing us from supposing God's works of power are only for those in a higher league than ours; and
- Freeing us to open to His grace-with-wonder-works in our own lives.

Elizabeth's "Blessed"

Let's look at the second time the phrase "blessed among women" occurs. It was spoken by Elizabeth almost immediately upon Mary's arrival at her cousin's home in Judea.

> Then she [Elizabeth] spoke out with a loud voice and said, "Blessed are you among women, and blessed is the fruit of your womb!" (Luke 1:42).

Back away a moment and take a full look, as well as a fresh one, at this part of the Gospel record.

Elizabeth is an older relative, who had only six months earlier conceived a later-in-life pregnancy. Now she and her husband, Zacharias, are awaiting the birth of their son — the child who will become John the Baptist, herald of the Messiah. But that's getting ahead of the story.

Two touchingly significant things can be captured at this point as the two women meet: the *wonder* and the *womanliness* being described.

1. The Wonder

Elizabeth has just received a Holy Spirit-inspired revelation of a wonder in process. She says so to Mary. In order to explain to the young girl her intuitive awareness of both Mary's pregnancy and its source, she exudes: "As soon as I heard your voice, the baby inside me leaped."[3]

In that same instant, Elizabeth was overflowed with the presence of the Holy Spirit. It is as though the child destined to point out the world's Savior had already begun his job! So Elizabeth's "blessed" isn't a deferring to Mary, but a declaring: "God just showed me that you're going to have a baby — and that your baby is the Messiah!"

Think now: Why did God give this insight to Elizabeth?

With the simplest reflection, unaffected by the impositions of human tradition, a very practical and gently gracious answer occurs. The Holy Spirit — the Helper always — is helping Mary at a moment she surely needed it.

Can you imagine Mary's thoughts, drawing near to Elizabeth's village of Ein Karem?

How can I explain what's begun in me? she wonders to herself. *Who will believe it?* But the answer was already on its way from heaven. Into the welter of Mary's very real human need for assistance and an understanding friend, the Spirit of God moved with a gentle grace. Elizabeth is informed by the Teacher, then filled with the Spirit and given to Mary as a friend in need.

Mary had come to visit and aid Elizabeth, but the older woman gets a head start on rendering loving service.

As we listen more closely to her words, we can see that Elizabeth isn't bowing before Mary. She is probably hugging her. Though awed by what God was doing in her young cousin, the older woman is more amazed at God's power than with Mary's presence; wondering over heaven's grace, right along with the miracle maiden herself.

So Elizabeth's prophecy was a confirmation, testifying to the fact Mary already knows but would be hard put to explain. She's relieving Mary of the burden of trying to describe the indescribable. It was God's way of removing any feeling from the virgin girl that she would be doubted when she said, "I'm pregnant, but, please believe me—I didn't do anything wrong!"

Elizabeth's prophecy was also an encouragement.

2. The Womanliness

The word "blessed," as we've noted before, is the
Greek *eulogeo* — "to speak well or approvingly of a
person." Elizabeth uses it twice: (1) in reference
to Mary, and (2) in speaking of the child within
her womb. Her intent is clear, when we allow ourselves to step back in time and to "feel" the
moment with those involved.

Mary had had several days to think on the
phenomenon that was taking place within her.
Undoubtedly, primary among her thoughts was
the inevitable question, *What will people think of me?*

Let's make no mistake about this. We're in the
middle of the most incredible wonder in universal
history — God becoming a man, and doing it in a
way that defies nature and, thereby, excites skep-
ticism. It is inescapable that this mode of heavenly entry will expose the vehicle of this wonder to
criticism, to inevitable unkind conclusions and
cynical comments. Yes, Mary, what *will* people
think?

But into this bewildering melee of thought,
Elizabeth's words come with a holy comfort and
assurance born of the same Holy Spirit who has
prompted her understanding by His gift of

prophecy. She says (and imagine her enfolding embrace as she speaks, bolstering Mary's trembling form):

"Young lady, God's going to take care of this situation. Don't you worry. In time, you're going to be spoken well of by other people who really understand. And so is that baby that's within you!"

That's what those words really say. They were words of "good," not words making Mary a god. Their meaning is warm and human, and miles removed from confusing tradition.

So is Elizabeth's following statement: "Why is the mother of my Lord coming here to see me?"[4] It was the most natural thing in the world for one pregnant woman to say to another.

Mary had just made a hard overland journey of more than 50 miles by ancient means of travel over bumpy roads. So Elizabeth's words are hardly an abject acknowledgement of some pretended superiority on Mary's part. Rather, they reveal the simple, forthright concern of a loving relative (a "Yiddisher Mama" kind of comment): "What are you doing, making such a trip here to see me—and in your condition?" *(Oi veh!)*

It is an exclamation, not a veneration. And, here again, the whole encounter draws us to see the genuinely "human" side rather than to invent a pretended "holy" side. Our removal of tradition's embellishments is a quest to assist us in unveiling God's glory in the everyday normal people's lives.

Let's keep at it by examining the third "blessed" that appears regarding Mary. Why bother? Because it is only by this "re-humanizing" study of the text that we can clearly gain a biblical perspective on our own candidacy for the Mary miracle.

Mary's "Blessed"

> For He [God] has regarded the lowly state of His maidservant; for behold, henceforth all generations will call me blessed. For He who is mighty has done great things for me,...And His mercy is on those who fear Him from generation to generation (Luke 1:48-50).

Let me emphasize it again. My earnest quest is to help us all see that while Mary certainly did have a marvelously significant role given her, and she was faithful to carry it through, she's also a picture of how God's great grace is ready to work the miraculous in every person. So in seeking to dissolve the obstacles of traditions that seem to move Mary's experience beyond our reach, I'm urging that we all expect our own Mary "kind" of miracles. That is actually the precise thing Mary was saying in her song when she bursts forth with the words: "In every generation I'll be called 'blessed.'" She is saying the same thing that everyone says when they see God's great goodness displayed toward them. This third time the word "blessed" appears in our text, a completely different Greek word occurs; different from Gabriel's greeting, and different from when Elizabeth was assuring Mary, "Be at peace. You'll not be unkindly spoken of." In this "blessed," Mary is talking about herself, and she says, "Everyone will say, I'm *makarios*!"

Nothing in the Greek word *makarios* recommends or hints that Mary thought any special acknowledgement would ever be due her. Rather, she's simply noting that people would understand and share her joy. The word means "happy, fortunate"—that is, blessed in the sense that "God has shown His kindness."

In short, this girl—amazed in the presence of God's grace—is saying, "Everyone who ever hears my story will say, 'That's one fortunate girl!'"

An Invitation to Us All

It's not hard to confirm that this was Mary's

thinking—far removed from her ever dreaming anyone would idolize her. Listen to the lyrics of the song she sings later. She declares the very same message I'm writing here, to persuade us all to accept: "His mercy (the same as shown to me) is ready to do similar great and mighty things from generation to generation—*whichever one you live in!*"[5]

Reread the text again, and let your heart leap with mine, dear one. Mary would surely want us to experience her joy because she recognized the Mary miracle was not intended to be confined to her, or its "kind" to happening only once!

I hope that by studying these three "blesseds" carefully, you sense the support of God's Word toward your own Mary miracle expectancy. Because we've secured solid terrain, grounding our faith in the unembellished truth of the Scriptures, we can open our hearts to God's won-der-promises with a clear-eyed perspective.

To summarize, then: (1) Gabriel's "Hail, Mary!" (see v. 28, *KJV*) with his "blessed are you," becomes easier to see for what it was—a warm greeting, not a promotion to a higher rung of humanity; (2) Elizabeth's "blessed" (see v. 42) was a comforting assurance to Mary, not an admiring adulation; and (3) Mary's "blessed" (see v. 48) was an invitation to us all to share her amazement.

So in these words we can hear the testimony of God's Word calling us to see the truth, the tenderness and the timelessness of God's grace:

- To see God's *truth*, which frees us to accept our uniqueness as Mary accepted hers;
- To see God's *tenderness*, in the way He moved Elizabeth by His Spirit, using her to comfort and assure Mary;
- To see God's *timelessness*, in the way He moved Mary to sing out the truth that her miracle was of an order that could have its own kind of realization in our generation, too.

But above all, let's lay hold of that third "blessed," realizing it is also Mary's invitation — no, it's *the Holy Spirit's!* It's His call through her song, calling every generation to humbly open themselves to the holy happiness she experienced. That one joyously fortunate person, who sang of the God whose miracle grace is available to us all, summons us today to open up to Him as she did.

But let us walk softly before God as we think on these things. Mary's response was amazement in God's presence. And it is into this same presence we are being ushered today, for those same mercies are promised from generation to generation.

Including ours.

꙳

CHAPTER SIX

The Issue of Innocence

Although Mary was as needy of the Savior as any of us, we know at least one noble thing about her, a trait that affirms the high quality of her character and lifestyle: She was a virgin.

Gabriel Sent to a Virgin

We're told, "The angel Gabriel was sent by God...to a virgin betrothed to a man whose name was Joseph,...The virgin's name was Mary" (Luke 1:26,27).

This issue of her sexual innocence is of enormous significance because, besides the necessity that the Messiah's mother be a Jewish girl, there was one other absolute requirement: She must be a virgin. There must be no question that the child born from her womb is entirely the product of God almighty's miracle working: *His* Son—God's, that is!

> Therefore the Lord Himself will give you a sign: Behold, the virgin shall conceive and bear a Son, and shall call His name Immanuel [God with us] (Isa. 7:14).

This prophecy was inscribed in the Holy Scriptures more than seven centuries before the Nazareth maiden was born: "There will come a day," the Spirit was saying, "when God shall become one *of* you, O mankind, and shall become one *with* you—Immanuel!" To mark the spiritual phenomenon of the infinite God becoming a finite man, Isaiah predicted a physical phenomenon would occur: "A virgin girl will bear the child."

Contrary to the prudish suppositions of some, this requirement of a virgin birth did not reflect a divine disapproval of normal sexual intercourse, as though it is a less than worthy way for a married couple to beget a child. Not at all. The procreative act of marriage—or, for that matter, the celebrative joy in married union (simply for pleasure)—was all God's idea from the beginning!

However, the virgin sign was absolute, being required by God to signal His divine intervention. The virgin birth is a miracle that not only reveals a wonder, but it also solves a basic problem: To become humankind's Savior, the Messiah must be of a new order.

- Only a "begotten Son of God," sired from outside Adam's race, yet begotten within it, could become the holy Lamb for sacrifice.
- Only God-become-flesh would be adequate to rewrite Genesis, to break the curse on Adam's seed and become the founder of the new creation—the second Adam.

Thus, a virginal candidate for this divine call to so supernatural a motherhood must be secured. Mary met this requirement, and that she had protected her virginity is certainly commendable. It seems to show evidence that Mary was probably a reverent, sensible young woman whose character and commitments moved her beyond any consideration of flirtatiousness or promiscuity.

On these grounds of conduct, it is also logical to conclude a number of other things were true

about Mary—devotion, responsibility, trustwor-
thiness and practical, homey intelligence. Because
God chose her to be the woman who would raise
His Son, it is reasonable to suppose she had more
worthwhile qualities than simply sexual purity.
But with specific reference to that most frequently mentioned characteristic of hers, we face a
problem. No, two problems.

The first is a religious problem of yet another
historic tradition; the second, a real problem of
occasional unspoken-but-real condemnation.

The Problem of Religious Tradition

First, we must address the religious tradition that
claims to teach "the perpetual virginity of Mary."
The idea this dogma proposes is that Mary not
only was a virgin when the Christ child was conceived, but also that she remained a virgin
throughout her lifetime. "Perpetual virginity"
argues that she and Joseph never consummated
their marriage, even after Jesus was born.

Notwithstanding several references to Jesus'
younger brothers and sisters (see Matt. 12:46;
Mark 6:3; John 2:12), a group of church leaders
created the concept of perpetual virginity nearly
600 years after the New Testament was complet-
ed. "After miraculously bearing God," they

announced, "it would have been incredible if Mary had then had sexual relations with Saint Joseph!"

Why?

There's no holy or human reason whatever for this proposal-come-lately, unless...unless, we're interested in building barriers to faith. Because such imaginary inventions do effectively erect walls.

The *∂e*-humanizing or *super*-humanizing of a person God has used militantly works against the possibility of expectant faith in others. Ordinary people dismiss hope, doubting that they might also be candidates for God's extraordinary graces.

But this tradition has neither a scriptural basis, nor is it theologically needed. It has served only to move Mary into an unreal world—out of the touchable realm of our personally identifying with her miracle.

And this is a problem. Because anything that confers something upon Mary that separates her from the kind of life normal people lead, becomes a blow to the Bible's beautiful message that God wants to work in every person the same kind of thing He worked in Mary.

• *He wants to beget Christ in us!*

I became a minister [to serve the

task]...given to me for you, to fulfill the word of God, the mystery...now...revealed to His saints....which is Christ in you, the

*A*NYTHING RENDERING US UNABLE TO FEEL AS PURE AS MARY, WILL EVENTUALLY PRODUCE A PSYCHOLOGY OF DESPAIR ABOUT GOD'S ABILITY TO USE US, OR TO CHANGE OUR WORLD BY SOMETHING HE MIGHT DO IN US.

hope of glory (Col. 1:25-27, italics added).

• *He wants to work glory within humanity!*

But we have this treasure in earthen ves-

sels [ordinary human bodies], that the
excellence of the power may be of God
and not of us (2 Cor. 4:7).

• *He is able to accomplish His will in and through us!*

For it is God who works in you both to
will and to do for His good pleasure
(Phil. 2:13).

The Problem of Condemnation

But, there is yet another problem besides the one
raised by religious tradition. When Mary's virginity is noted, especially because it was a requirement for her being used by God, an unspoken, yet
very real, personal blockage to simple faith may
often surface.

Too readily, the spirit of condemnation can
assail and oppose the spirit of expectancy. With
understandable ease, one's personal possibilities
in God's will become blurred by doubt, as any one
of us could be tempted to argue: "My sins—especially sins of lust, whether imaginary or actual—
clearly disqualify me for the Mary miracle."

In effect, anything rendering us unable to feel
as pure as Mary will eventually produce a psychology of despair about God's ability to use us,

or to change our world by something He might do in us. A binding sense of intimidation cripples multitudes. Whether our failure has been through sexual disobedience to God's laws, or any other area of violated purity for that matter, a crushing blow to triumphant faith can too quickly be registered.

Sadly, a person's holy respect for righteousness becomes an unholy removal from the belief that God can work wonders in him or her. But in contrast to this, the Mary miracle is meant to teach us all: Your holy Father is ready to bring wonders *to* you, to work them *in* you, that *through* you He might change the world *around* you!

Then, if the Mary miracle requires a virgin for its introduction, is it possible we are living in a dreamworld to think such miracle works are available to us? Isn't it more logical to adopt the human reasoning that asks:

> Doesn't God work only through perfect people—"saints" of accomplished spirituality? "Immaculately conceived" people who are divinely destined to be exceptions? Transcendent, spiritual royalty beyond us "normal people" who were designed only as pawns, not queens or kings?

Or to insist:

> How can people who live in the sweat and
> stew of an unclean society attain to such
> faith as Mary's? Doesn't her perpetual
> self-denial of her humanity—never tast-
> ing the physical joys of marriage—prove
> that she and her miracle are outside the
> scope of most everyone else's expecta-
> tions?

The issue of innocence is a formidable one. It
can't be lightly dismissed because it *is* true that
the Mary model reveals that Mary miracles man-
date virginal candidates. And whether our human
failures are attitudinal or actual, mental or physical, social or private, sexual or otherwise, we are
all sinners with the voice of guilt dictating doubt
to our souls: "Forget it, you're no Saint Mary!"

Of course, that is true. Only one person in history was Mary of Nazareth, but that isn't the
point. There is not a need for a precise repeat of
that Mary, because none of us are called to be
vehicles of the same miracle she experienced. We
are called only to the same *order* of divine possibilities happening in us.

Further, the power that enabled Mary to experience her miracle was not given or assisted by

some self-accrued saintliness, nor by her virginity. The entirety of the extraordinary thing God did in her was produced by His promise and His power. And it is the same promised power by which He confers sainthood today.

God makes saints, not by ecclesiastical edict, but through the righteousness of His Son Jesus Christ, a perfect wholeness and holiness He attributes by *His* edict. He confers this upon failures who come to Him with faith in the Savior alone, and it is this faith that can still qualify anyone as a candidate for the Mary miracle. It not only lifts the most common or corrupt sinner to instant, heaven-authenticated sainthood, but it also restores virginity where it has been lost.

Meet Saint Theodore.

❧

CHAPTER SEVEN

Saint Theodore

Ted was sorely disturbed.

The fact that he was already a seasoned believer, having walked with Christ for more than ten years, seemed to make little difference in his ability to deal with a major obstacle in his life path. The day he stepped into my office for counsel he was not being superficial or emotionally exaggerative. He had thought and tried, long and hard. His description of his problem, and the accompanying despair he felt, was neither a mock-pious ranting nor a self-induced guilt trip.

A Godly — Yet Tormented — Man

"Pastor," he began, "I frankly doubt that I can

ever become the man God wants me to be. I wouldn't bother you with dramatics—I mean this. I've asked to talk to you only because it seems I've gotten nowhere at every point of effort in prayer and the Word.

"You see," he continued, "I've wrestled for so long—fought with something that isn't easy to confess. Even though I haven't entertained carnal habits, the problem nags me relentlessly, dragging my mind down and my heart to hopelessness.

"The problem is simply this: Even though I haven't and won't give place to unfaithfulness in my marriage, and even though I don't indulge in pornography, I still struggle constantly with foul, pornographic thoughts."

Most frustrating to him was the fact that, even though he had not been indulgent to the sins his mind called him to, he couldn't seem to escape the thoughts. He was a godly man, living a committed life of godliness, yet tormented to the point of near despair by a sexual pollution that, unfed, still dominated his mind.

Ted felt like anything but a saint, and even less like a candidate for a belief that God could do anything through him—then or ever. For him, the problem of foulmindedness constituted a kind of "lost virginity," if you will.

In other words, a Mary "kind" of miracle—of

Christ's promise and power changing his world —
seemed out of the question. For his part, his
struggle certainly removed the likelihood of his
ever being a person to and through whom God's
promise and power could flow. Maybe God's
mercy would be his with the hope of heaven
someday, but he had concluded, "Forget anything
about God's mightiness in my life here on earth!"

I felt the man's weariness, the long struggle of
a dedicated disciple. But it was clear that spiritual sincerity and pursued purity weren't gaining
the victory he sought. Then, as we talked, the
Holy Spirit prompted me.

"Ted, you know me well enough to know that
the question I'm about to ask would never be
made for any cheap reason of carnal curiosity.
But let me put it bluntly: Are there any incidents
of specific physical sexual immorality in your
past? I mean, prior to your marriage and your
commitment to our Lord Jesus?"

He turned away, his eyes cast downward for a
moment. Then he slowly looked up, squarely into
my eyes, and what followed was a forthright,
frank confession. There had been several
instances of fornication while he was in college.
One resulted in his financing an abortion for the
coed he had impregnated.

Through misty eyes, he told me two things.

First, he said he knew he had long since been for-given for these sins. Ted clearly understood that when he received Christ as his Savior, God's grace had washed the record clean in heaven's eyes. Whatever his struggle, it wasn't due to a shallow interpretation of God's grace given to him in salvation.

But there was a second thing, something piv-otal in his tenderhearted response. It indicated to me that the very matter we were touching on was somehow key to his sought-for release as both of us sensed a "witness" that the Holy Spirit had brought us to the crux of the problem. We were not dealing with either a negligent disciple or an indulgent man, but with a point of bondage—an unholy spirit, taunting a forgiven soul.

What followed as we prayed together was not to gain a deeper forgiveness. We cannot improve on the fullness of the acquittal from all our sin that we receive when we open our lives to the sav-ing grace of God through the blood of Jesus' cross. However, many believers never enter into a distinct and glorious arena of deliverance until they confront the lying works of darkness that sometimes plague the redeemed.

I have often discovered that the residue of a person's past sins, though forgiven by God, can still somehow lurk in the soul, like rubbish swept under a rug, or garbage crammed in a corner and rotting. Such "collections" all too easily become a breeding place for the flies of hell—Beelzebub's minions. Where the past festers in this way, however greatly heaven's forgiveness may have been accomplished, something is still souring a soul on earth.

Released from the Enemy's Lies

In Ted's case, these evil assaults were succeeding because of a lingering sense of unworthiness—an undefined, yet no less present, subtle suggestion: "Sure, you're forgiven! But you've still sinned so far beyond the ordinary that the possibilities of God's best purposes for your life will never be realized."

When this kind of mind-set haunts a person, even the most mature believer is often stunted; but young, inexperienced believers seem completely suffocated. Given time, lying spirits will persuade your soul:

- You deserve less than God's best anyhow, so just consider yourself lucky to be going to heaven and skip dreams of dynamic attainment on earth.
- You would be more honest to simply give

up (maybe even take your life and rid earth of such a blockage to others as you are). Come on—get honest with the facts. You're hopeless, limited, through!

In such situations, the only things that seem unlimited are the litany of lies concocted when the Lord of the Flies sets the soul buzzing with battering doubts. But for such struggles a place of refuge and rest can be found. It is found in applying the power principle that releases that order of healing James describes:

> Confess your trespasses to one another, and pray for one another, that you may be healed. The effective, fervent prayer of a righteous man avails much (Jas. 5:16).

On the basis of this and other Scriptures, I led Ted in a time of prayer. Every aspect of the past, and the lies that had attached to it, were all brought under the cover of Christ's blood. We prayed that the blood that had already reconciled Ted to our Father in heaven would now work its soul-releasing power over the demonic bonds seeking to restrain him on earth.

As we invited the claims of Calvary, a holy power was unleashed that hell's condemnation

could not withstand. The fruit of Ted's breakthrough was:

- A new sense of joy in his life;
- A complete overthrow of evil thoughts;
- A bright expectancy of God's expanding
  purpose in and through his life—both at
  home and professionally.

It happened. His own Mary miracle was "conceived" in Ted shortly thereafter, and today he is
one of the most effective men I know. And he is as
free and fruitful in every part of his life—voca-
tionally and domestically—as in his service for
Christ. But as marvelous as the new beginnings
(or make that "new begettings") in Ted's experience have become, I don't know anyone who calls
him Saint Theodore. Except God.

God Calls Us "Saints"!

You are aware of that, aren't you? The Almighty
God, who alone dwells in perfect holiness and
righteous splendor, calls the most ordinary people
"saints." The word means "holy ones," which
makes His designation all the more amazing, seeing that the best among us are considerably short
of Webster's demanding definition of "holy":

- "Exalted or worthy of complete devotion as one perfect in goodness and righteousness";
- "Divine, or having a divine quality."

These words describe something, or someone, quite beyond that "ordinary person" description I have given for potential Mary miracle candidates; for people through whom Mary's kind of blessing multiplies. And it is precisely this definition that discourages hope in so many saints, causing some to think, *Back away quick, before you're duped by the devil into believing too much of yourself!*

But the truth in God's Word shows that He does use that term over and over to describe all of us who have become open to His love:[1]

> Gather My saints together to Me, those who have made a covenant with Me by sacrifice. Let the heavens declare His righteousness, for God Himself is Judge (Ps. 50:5,6).

This ancient song peals forth the grounds for God's unabashed willingness to call people like us "saints."

First, it is because they have sealed a

"covenant"—a contracted arrangement with Him "by sacrifice." Second, it is because this agreement fully answers to, and aligns with, His standard of righteousness. Thus, as the senior and overruling Judge of the entire universe, His declaration stands above all: "They're saints!"

That's you and me He is talking about, loved one! And, of course, the sacrifice accomplishing this transaction is the death of Jesus Christ upon the cross (2 Cor. 5:17,19,21):

- *He made us entirely new!*

    Therefore, if anyone is in Christ, he is a new creation; old things have passed away; behold, all things have become new.

- *Our past record is entirely cleared!*

    God was in Christ reconciling the world to Himself, not imputing [or, placing to their account] their trespasses.

- *Christ's holiness is entirely ours!*

    He made Him [Jesus, His Son] who knew

no sin to be sin for us, that we might
become the righteousness of God in Him
[that is, through placing our trust for forgiveness in Jesus Christ].

The summary conclusion in the court deposi-
tion God has placed permanently in His own
heavenly files is this: The sinlessly perfect record
of His Son Jesus has been transferred to our personal account!

This is the reason God cannot only keep a
straight face when He calls us "My holy ones,"
but also in declaring it, He moves right ahead to
offering all the possibilities one would expect
might become available to a child of creation's
Maker and salvation's King!

A Faith-Liberating Hope

To these truths, let me add another marvel.
There's a Bible lesson in the restorative powers of
this "sainting" God confers with His complete
forgiveness of our sins. What I want us to see
often escapes some eyes because it seems almost
too glorious to believe. But we must both *see* and
believe it. It is uniquely essential for us in this particular study because through the deep failure of
a certain group of people in the Bible, then

through their full restoration, a faith-liberating hope can distill in our souls.

Look with me at some men and women whose experience can assure us that the possibilities of Mary's miracle still apply to us, however tarnished our past.

THE MARY MIRACLE—

WITH ITS SEEDS OF PROMISE—

OPENED THE WAY TO TED'S

BECOMING THE MAN HE WAS FIRST

CREATED TO BE, AND THEN

REDEEMED TO BECOME.

❧

It was from Corinth, the city in the ancient Roman world that was so sexually perverted and corrupted through every imaginable indulgence, that the word "corinthian" derived to become the globally employed adjective for "rotten to the core."

Paul had brought the gospel of Christ to that place, and in writing his first letter to them years later, he remembers what they had been *before*, and what they had now *become* in Christ. He lists their past misdeeds: fornicators, idolaters, adulterers, homosexuals, sodomites, thieves, insatiably indulgent, drunkards, troublemakers, extortioners.

After reiterating the memory of this history of their having formerly wallowed in our virtual cesspool of human failures, he asserts again, "And such were some of you." Then, in one grand sweep of the pen, he declares, "But you were *washed*, but you were *sanctified*, but you were *justified* [i.e., declared completely 'not guilty!'] in the name of the Lord Jesus."[2]

Astounding! Notwithstanding everything less than "virginal" in their behavior, he declares the gospel truth: "You're washed clean now!" All this would be wonderful enough, just on the terms of this glorious grace of God to so completely forgive. But in his second letter to the Corinthians, Paul makes an even more astonishing statement.

To these Corinthians, so many of whom had been so deeply scarred by sin at so many grotesque points of extreme impurity, the apostle writes again: "For I am jealous for you with a godly jealousy. For I have betrothed [promised or engaged] you to one husband [the Savior], that I may present you as a chaste virgin to Christ" (2 Cor. 11:2).

Do you hear that, dear one? *A chaste virgin.* Look at this awesome new creation statement in God's Word! See how former sin and sex addicts are now being declared "virginal!" Can you imagine a more towering statement on how vast the possibilities of God's restorative powers are, once He sets about recovering ruined, broken or sin-stained people?

Of course, the text isn't suggesting a physical restoration of the human hymen, the membrane that is torn in a woman's body the first time sexual intercourse occurs. Rather, Paul is testifying to people of both genders, men and women alike, telling them, "God's Spirit is able to bring back that pure, simple and childlike quality of soul to you; to renew you so completely that your heart becomes like a virgin's so that your life and your love can belong to your Lord completely, and without shame, fear or doubt!"

So it was with Ted.

"Yessir, Theodore," God might have said that day, "I'm ready to birth a new freedom through you." The Mary miracle is as fully available to a man who had fornicated, and then financed his conquest's abortion, as it was to the sexually untainted virgin in Nazareth.

Because of Ted's commitment to trust in Jesus as His Savior, he was regarded as unconditionally accepted, forgiven and holy in the eyes of heaven. And when he saw how eternal reality opened the promise of temporal victory, he became pregnant!

The Mary miracle—with its seeds of promise—opened the way to Ted's becoming the man he was first created to be, and then redeemed to become.

The promise of the Mary miracle is equally available at any point in life to any person on earth who believes, then becomes open: anyone who believes in Jesus Christ as God's Son, the resurrected Savior, and then opens up to the unfolding possibilities the Father offers.

Whatever the problem facing you, whatever the fear that entraps, the doubt that plagues, the relationship that is weakened, the hope that is fleeing, the dream or desire that seems beyond reach—"saints" can receive the birthing of something new.

But you have to become pregnant first.

❧

PART 3

The Way Miracles Happen

AND THE ANGEL ANSWERED AND SAID TO HER:

"THE HOLY SPIRIT WILL COME UPON YOU, AND THE

POWER OF THE HIGHEST WILL OVERSHADOW YOU;

THEREFORE, ALSO, THAT HOLY ONE WHO IS TO BE BORN

WILL BE CALLED THE SON OF GOD."—LUKE 1:35

Religious tradition often processes miracles as artifacts of the past; defined and defended so as to prevent the possibility of our expecting one today—or *every* day, for that matter.

THEN THE ANGEL SAID TO HER, "DO NOT BE AFRAID, MARY, FOR YOU HAVE FOUND FAVOR WITH GOD. AND BEHOLD, YOU WILL CONCEIVE IN YOUR WOMB AND BRING FORTH A SON, AND SHALL CALL HIS NAME JESUS. HE WILL BE GREAT, AND WILL BE CALLED THE SON OF THE HIGHEST; AND THE LORD GOD WILL GIVE HIM THE THRONE OF HIS FATHER DAVID. AND HE WILL REIGN OVER THE HOUSE OF JACOB FOREVER, AND OF HIS KINGDOM THERE WILL BE NO END."

THEN MARY SAID TO THE ANGEL, "HOW CAN THIS BE, SINCE I DO NOT KNOW A MAN?"

AND THE ANGEL ANSWERED AND SAID TO HER: "THE HOLY SPIRIT WILL COME UPON YOU, AND THE POWER OF THE HIGHEST WILL OVERSHADOW YOU; THEREFORE, ALSO, THAT HOLY ONE WHO IS TO BE BORN WILL BE CALLED THE SON OF GOD. NOW INDEED, ELIZABETH YOUR RELATIVE HAS ALSO CONCEIVED A SON IN HER OLD AGE; AND THIS IS NOW THE SIXTH MONTH FOR HER WHO WAS CALLED BARREN. FOR WITH GOD NOTHING WILL BE IMPOSSIBLE."

THEN MARY SAID, "BEHOLD THE MAIDSERVANT OF THE LORD! LET IT BE TO ME ACCORDING TO YOUR WORD."

LUKE 1:30-38

CHAPTER EIGHT

The Things Angels Say

We hadn't planned on this baby. But there's an inescapable law of married love that, if you are open to its expression, life has a way of multiplying. And love, too. Love was shortly to be written all over the three little faces in front of us.

Anna and I had called the kids into the living room after the supper dishes were washed. They hadn't expected much more than a brief family meeting of sorts—a review of something we would be doing that weekend, or an item of relatively small significance. But there was more in store for us all than any of them imagined.

"Kids," I began, "Mom and I want to take a

few minutes and talk about something that is going to happen because we know you'll all want to know before we tell anyone else."

They didn't have the slightest anticipation of the unusual. The youngest was seven years old, and along with his nine-year-old brother and eleven-year-old sister, they had concluded what Anna and I had previously believed: We had finished our family. But that had all changed now.

We were all seated on the floor, in front of the old heater that was made a little more elegant by having had a mantle built around it. It was early autumn, school had resumed and homework was waiting when I finished talking to them so I got right to the point. Reaching over to take Anna's hand, I smiled and said to the trio, "Mama's going to have a baby."

The room became electric. Big sister Becki's face broke into a slow-grow smile that seemed to stretch from wall to wall. Jack looked stunned, and his small hand opened as he brought it upward and slapped his forehead as though to say, "I can't believe it!" Mark's eyes, then his voice, spoke his puzzlement: "I thought Mom was too old to have any more babies."

And for our part, though still in our early thirties we had been as surprised a few weeks before as our kids were now.

That pleasant memory is a generation behind us today because that baby—our daughter Christa—is now married and has a brand-new baby of her own, born last Thanksgiving Day. But the joy of that memory goes well beyond the initial surprise Anna and I experienced, or that realized by our children.

Christa's birth—which was a welcome addition, but hardly a convenience to our carefully laid plans—became a practical lesson in the wisdom of God's planning as opposed to ours: "For as the heavens are higher than the earth, so are My ways higher than your ways, and My thoughts than your thoughts" (Isa. 55:9).

Little did we know how that baby was given to signal an entirely new era in our lives. For she had hardly been born when the Holy Spirit began to stir us toward new pathways. They opened through a Holy Spirit-directed turn that resulted in our accepting an obscure little pastorate in the San Fernando Valley, which eventually became The Church On The Way. Our joyous acceptance of an unexpected pregnancy became the launching point of a continual flow of wonders.

"Surprise Babies"

Looking back on it, I can't escape the feeling that

the two events were linked in God's plan for us. It's as though He was testing our willingness to allow Him to upset our plans and set His in motion at a new dimension of miracle wonder.

How likely is it that, even as you read this, the Father has a "surprise baby" for you—I mean, a new turn with wonders waiting ahead?

I know this: Whatever His promises for your future may be, two things are certain about it.

First, they are good: "For I know the thoughts that I think toward you, says the Lord, thoughts of peace and not of evil, to give you a future and a hope" (Jer. 29:11).

Second, His promises work only in, and through, those who are willing to become "pregnant." (In fact, I think it's time to confess to you that my heart's purpose in writing this book is in the hope that the largest possible number of people will do just that—"get pregnant," I mean.)

Of course, this order of pregnancy is subject to any number of definitions in its *out*working. But at the point of its *in*working, it begins with our personal heart-readiness to be open to God's call.

Answering that call leads the way to His loving purpose, to His living promise and to His transforming power. But I have found that most of us open only to the degree that we trust Him, and answer only to the degree that we believe He is committed to bless our lives, not mess them up.

God's Call to You

Gabriel's visit to Mary issued the heavenly Father's invitation. And the things the angel said were laden with hope for Mary's world and for glory to fill the future. Listen to these phrases because the things angels say give us a clue to God's way of thinking when He calls us to His purposed plan for our lives.

- He will be great (Luke 1:32).
- The Lord God will give Him the throne (Luke 1:32).
- Of His kingdom there will be no end (Luke 1:33).

I can't urge you strongly enough to let these words settle into your own soul because, like the Mary miracle, they also are a genre—a "kind" of thing God does. Although they were spoken of Jesus, whom Mary would bear, the truer-than-ever truth today is that this same Jesus has come to dwell in us. And the purpose of His entry is not only to abide *with* us, but also to extend His kingdom *through* us.

So many dear believers only think of this

"extending" in terms of religious duties, accepting Christian disciplines and trying harder to "be good." Thus, attempting to master our limitations and trying to cultivate self-discipline becomes a wearying effort at spiritual achievement. But our Father's plan is to birth Christ's life *in* us, not demand His life *from* us.

I have an angelic "word" for you about this, the same one spoken by the shepherds: "Today a Savior is born to you."[1] There's a new life resource available for every new day, and a new challenge, too. God wants to reveal His "surprise" workings at new dimensions of joy we couldn't have thought possible. Whether you're seeking to respond to His call to a new realm of service, or trying to overcome an old problem that has caused stress for you, I invite you to "listen to the angels."

This Mary-miracle approach to growth and victory isn't painless or problem-free—having babies never is. But it is alive and aglow, filled with joy, rather than with juggling the metallic pieces of a "Do-It-Yourself Christian Kit." God's surprise ways are superior to our best efforts at *anything*—even trying to live for Him. He is in the life-begetting, birthing business because it produces sons and daughters, not robots.

The good news of the gospel doesn't end with our new birth. It continues by announcing the possibilities of periodic, additional surprise babies—birthings of blessing making possible new growth, and always through the power of new grace. Such a life-flow to us, in us and through us changes things around us as we find:

- Release from life's most besetting sin, as habits are broken and forgiveness drives out guilt;
- Brightness shining in life's darkest corners, as love beams in and drives out fear;
- Provision unfolds for life's deepest need, as God's abundance drives out want;
- Strength flows to focus on life's weakest point, as divine enablement drives out failure;
- Health springs forth at life's sorest place, as the Healer Himself begins to drive out pain.

Listen to the Angels

The Mary miracle is the means by which these possibilities are conceived. But a healthy impregnation requires, first, that we listen to the angels; that we tune in to the real message that comes from God's throne. It hasn't changed.

If anything is consistent about the revelation

of God's reaching toward us, it's the reality of the ceaseless flow of love He extends to us all. Angels declare it:

- Angels come to Abraham and Sarah to tell them that the child they have always wanted, and have been unable to conceive, will be forthcoming (see Gen. 18:1-15).
- Angels appear to Jacob, ascending and descending a ladder, linking heaven and earth, and he receives God's sure promise for his future (see Gen. 28:10-22).
- The angel goes before the people of Israel during their wilderness journey to take them to their appointed destination and inheritance (see Exod. 23:20-33).
- The Angel of the Lord comes to Gideon at a time he is hiding for fear in seclusion and declares to him God's high purpose and destiny for his life (see Judg. 6:11-23).
- An angel comes to Daniel and, in response to the man's impassioned prayer, brings a prophetic word laden with hope and future promise (see Dan. 10:1-21).
- The Angel of the Lord joins the three Hebrew children in the midst of the fiery furnace, bringing deliverance and vindicating their cause (see Dan. 3:24-28).

- An angel comes to Peter after Herod had locked him in the innermost prison, and miraculously leads the way through a series of obstacles to freedom (see Acts 12:6-11).
- An angel appears to Paul, tempest-tossed on the high seas of a Mediterranean winter storm, and assures him that his life will be spared and his trip will be successful (see Acts 27:23,24).
- Angels bring messages of Christ's ultimate victory to John, as he serves his unjustly ascribed sentence on the Isle of Patmos, and Jesus visits him, bringing peace and promise (see Rev. 1:9-20; 19:9,10; 22:6).

Listen, loved one. Listen to God's word to you, because His Spirit is still breathing messages today as He whispers words to your soul.

Angel messages more frequently come through the Holy Spirit's ministry today, either by prophetic gift, vital preaching, personal promptings or devotional reading of the Scriptures. But they say the same wonderful things as they always have. Why? Because God is the same Lover, Comforter, Friend and Creator of His "good things" for His children as He has always been.

God wants His message of encouragement to get through to us because otherwise our minds become deafened by the roar of circumstance, and our hearts close up to hope. But God's Word—brought by the messages spoken to us in the quiet of our hearts, the silence of our room or by any of the dozens of means He may employ to get His Word to us—*that* Word is calling you and me to hear, and to be open to love's promise of hope, whatever our situation.

What are you facing, or walking through, that needs heaven's promise spoken—then born into the middle of it?

Go back a moment and look at the nine examples previously listed, cases in which angels spoke and brought the word of God's will and promise. You will notice that every one of them has a practical point of application today, and it is not playing games to see comparisons. God wants us to see these incidents and know that they are intended to be viewed as windows through which we see His ways—then believe His promises.

> For whatever things were written before were written for our learning, that we through the patience and comfort of the Scriptures might have hope (Rom. 15:4).

The words the angels spoke in ancient days were written to speak to us. They tell us that God wants to:

1. Fulfill our longings;
2. Secure our future;
3. Give confident direction;
4. Stimulate a godly self-image;
5. Point to a brighter tomorrow;
6. Bring us through life's fire;
7. Free us from life's prisons;
8. Take us safely through life's storms;
9. Bring us to ultimate victory.

That's the kind of hope and promise God wants people to hear and receive. Angels know that, too.

If Mary had asked, would anyone have said to her, "Listen to the angels, girl"?

Probably not.

But because Mary listened to the angel, she became pregnant with the Greatest Promise in the world Who answered all humankind's need and still satisfies every person's thirst for forgiveness, meaning and destiny. The Mary miracle, then, points a pathway for recurrent promise to come into actual experience: You begin by listening, receiving the message of hope and believing the promise:

He [Christ in you] will be great [that is, meet and exceed all expectations] (Luke 1:32).

The Lord God [who created you] will give Him the throne [that is, Jesus' presence and power to rule over all that opposes you] (Luke 1:32).

Of His kingdom [which is the manifest ruling grace of God in your life, expelling what seeks to defeat or discourage you] there will be no end [because He has come to stay, not to tease you with samples] (Luke 1:33).

Birthing Greatness Out of Garbage

I first met Phil at the airport lounge while I was waiting for a flight to Europe. We never became well acquainted, but I had occasion to speak to him three or four times in the season following that first encounter.

The first time we met he was rather bashful and retiring, far from assertive, because our meeting had occurred when he recognized me from my appearances on television. He didn't want to seem as though he were a teenager, gushing over a sports figure or entertainer. However, he did give me a gift—a very simple, inexpensive one, but he briefly explained its meaning to him, which made the small token a priceless thoughtfulness to me.

Some time later I had the opportunity for a longer conversation with Phil. That is the day he "told it all," so to speak.

"Pastor Jack," he smiled, "I hope you won't misunderstand my happiness in having the opportunity to talk with you, even though this is brief, and our contacts are rare. But I have to tell you something, because you're more important to where I am in my life than you can possibly know."

Being a rather short man with a very unassuming presence, I returned his smile and reached over to put my hand on his shoulder, as if to say, "Be comfortable, friend. Go ahead." But, actually, I remained silent and just listened.

"You see, Pastor," he began, then his eyes teared slightly, "I'm a garbage man."

Phil tried to blink back the tears, then chuckled self-consciously. "Don't get me wrong," he explained, while wiping his eyes, "I'm not crying because I'm a garbage collector."

Now he began to wipe his glasses with a handkerchief, as he went on. "I actually do quite well, and I'm sure you think no less of me because of my profession."

Glasses back in place, with eyes dried but shining, he continued. "But there's something about the fact of my work that made me think less of myself than I realized. I would have denied it, but it was the truth. I didn't think of myself as having real significance, other than simply making it through from day to day.

"Yeah, I knew the Lord—but then, that was a ticket to heaven. But I never really caught the picture of who God saw me to be, and how great His purposes for my life were now, until I began tuning in to your broadcast."

Then he looked straight at me, having the unaffected yet mighty bearing of a royal heir. "Jack, Jesus used you to help Ephesians 1:18 become mine! The eyes of my understanding [heart] became enlightened like the sun shining at full strength, and I could see myself the way Father God sees me. It changed my life."

The man was majesty in a sports shirt, royalty in a pair of denim jeans. He finished with these words.

"I've heard you enough to know you, and I realize you understand the way I mean this because you're wise enough to know it's God who does it all. But you, Pastor Jack, were the voice of God to me, telling me His message and helping me learn how to open to it. Like I said, it changed my life; I've already thanked God for that. But I just wanted a chance to thank you, too."

My emotions were spongy by now and my eyes were also glistening, as were his. "I do

THE ANGEL'S WORDS HAD INTRODUCED RUMORS OF GREATNESS, PROMISED BY HEAVEN TO EARTHLINGS WHO WILL RECEIVE THE IMPREGNATING HOPE THAT BIRTHS GOD'S KINGDOM POSSIBILITIES WITHIN THEM.

understand, Phil. And I do thank you, too. Thank you for letting His promises inside so they could multiply, and keep passing what He multiplies on to others."

I hugged him. And as I did, I felt a slight

tremor of emotion go through a man who, as I later learned, had had most of his personhood ripped out through tough times in his early life and painful relationships later.

But Phil was pregnant—I could tell. The Mary miracle was birthing greatness out of the garbage, and the fragrance of Christ's person in this man was beautifully in evidence.

In effect, Phil had called me an angel—a messenger bringing God's hope, promise and purpose to him; speaking the truth that there is a power that can change everything, recover everyone and bring God's victory every time.

He had listened, and the "angel's" words had introduced rumors of greatness, promised by heaven to earthlings who will receive the impregnating hope that births God's kingdom possibilities within them.

"Surprise babies" of the Father's loving purpose are waiting to be born. The Mary miracle starts with word of their availability for birth. But their begetting requires more than a promise.

Their conception also needs life-giving power.

❧

CHAPTER NINE

How in the World?

The word "conceive" is used in two ways in the English language: (1) to become pregnant, and (2) to imagine or receive an idea or opinion. Whether mentioning a baby in the womb or a military bomber on the drawing board, both are referred to as having been conceived.

The word "deliver" is also employed in at least two ways: (1) to describe giving birth to a child, and (2) to declare the setting free of a person or creature.

Understanding Life Through the Mary Miracle

It seems more than accidental that these two terms, "conceive" and "deliver," converge in the two parts of the human anatomy that convey life: the heart and the womb. We conceive in both, and we deliver from both.

Conception. People are said to conceive ideas or plans in their hearts, even though their minds may be involved. Proverbs 23:7 says that the way a man thinks in his heart is the way he really is, and the fruit of what he *allows to enter* his being attitudinally. Paralleling this, babies are the natural biological result of sexual union; that is, they too are the fruit of what is *allowed to enter* the womb physiologically.

Delivery. We deliver from both the heart and the womb as well. Matthew 12:34 notes, "For out of the abundance of the heart the mouth speaks." Further, we not only deliver the content of our hearts, we also have the capacity to deliver souls, as our hearts dispense love, life and salvation through our witness. Then again, in the parallel point of the physical realm, common parlance will announce the arrival of a newborn infant, saying, "She was 'delivered' at 8:13 P.M."

The point in making these simple observations on word usage is that they illustrate how commonly our culture integrates the biological/physical realm with the psychological/spiritual realm. Our paralleling them in analogy is neither a strained nor a belabored exercise. To join the two, as we are doing in our discussion of the Mary miracle, is consistent with the ways we think and live and express ourselves, whether we have noticed it before or not.

To put it succinctly, everything about life that is fruitful, multiplying or creatively reproductive and fulfilling is discussed the same way. We conceive and we deliver; we receive the seed of an *idea* or the sperm begetting a *child* and, in either case, life is freed or fruitful at new dimensions.

To understand the Mary miracle is to understand life. It's to understand how you and I can move beyond whatever might limit our capacity to become partners with our heavenly Father in opening our beings to His creative power as well as His redeeming grace. Mary's miracle is vital to our understanding and application because it displays the principles by which God's holy power can be introduced into humble human situations; how God's creative and redemptive grace uses people like us to accomplish heaven's purposes and possibilities — on earth. So "how in the world" can we realize these possibilities, seeing our own human limits?

We Live in a Power-Hungry World

No amount of human enterprise seems too great to expend in the quest of greater power. An

Alexander or a Napoleon will marshal armies; a maddened Hitler will savage a continent and assail an ancient people group; a Dillinger will machine gun associates as well as adversaries; a whole planet will pursue nuclear dominance at almost any cost.

On the other hand, when technology, finance or military might become disinteresting or incapable of satisfying man's power thirst, the more desperate and deceived will turn to the spiritually evil or the occult. People will cultivate black arts, seek mind control, traffic with demons and consult dark powers. Whether they seek power through war or warlocks, the end result is inevitably the same: Humankind's power quests always end in bondage, slavery, destruction and, ultimately, death.

Enter the girl from Nazareth.

In Mary, the God who created us all with a hunger for meaning (a hunger so often diverted to the quest of might) provided the possibility of true fulfillment and satisfaction. It would start in the child Mary conceived and delivered, for He would provide humankind with the way out of the death trap of eternal loss. And it is in Mary that God also unveiled the pattern by which we can be freed from the life trap of human power-lessness.

That void of power—of "freeing, delivering power"—is what so many sense, and it's what causes us to crave carnal substitutes. The quest for gaining better control of our situation, of our environment, of our relationships, leads multitudes down numberless blind alleys in the power search for some way to make things work.

Enter the dove from heaven.

It's ironic. God has ordained that our ultimate lesson in finding and understanding the power we need for successful living converges in a mere girl and a gentle dove. Once again, we discover how God's ways defy our systems, and how His mind denies our suppositions. So it is, God calls us all to Nazareth to learn about life, about power and about how all of it works.

How Can This Be?

We're now at the point where Gabriel has announced the purpose of this divine visitation, and Mary is marveling at God's mercifulness. But, being so familiar with the script, most of us too quickly run past what would have been an absolute enigma to her. We have read the story, but she hadn't. And right now her head is spinning with a basic question, just as her heart is with an overwhelming sense of God's grace.

Pardon me, Mr. Angel. I hope I don't seem ignorant or irreverent for asking, but how in the world—in this one where I live—how can these things be? Especially, sir, since, as you know, I've never been with a man. Exactly, please, how do I have this baby?

I have taken some liberties with the actual text, of course. But I think, given the unprecedented and unimaginable situation Mary was facing, it's possible her mind tumbled with a few more thoughts than she put to speech. I also have a purpose in my elaboration of Mary's supposed thoughts.

Hardly a day goes by that I don't talk with someone who sounds very much as I have suggested Mary might have thought, people who relate almost exactly as Mary did to the angel.

- That's a worthwhile project, Jack, but I don't know that I have what it takes to get it done.

- Yes, Pastor. I know that's the way I should handle my responses when my husband [or wife] says [or does] that. But I don't have the patience [or trust, or heart, or willpower].

- Sure, I know that's the way to look at the

problem, and I do believe God's Word shows the answer. But, honestly, I just don't think I have the faith.

- The whole thing has been on my back so long, I'm ready to give up. It's more than I ever imagined, and I've decided it's sure more than I can stand.

And the beat goes on—people "beat up" with life and feeling whipped because "I don't have what it takes."

So we return to Mary and Gabriel and the angel's next words. Because what God's messenger from heaven said that day to a questioning girl is the one answer capable of providing the power needed to resolve or transform any human dilemma. When Mary asked, "How can these things be?" the angel replied:

> The Holy Spirit will come upon you, and the power of the Highest will overshadow you (Luke 1:35).

These words give the one sufficient and satisfying resource capable both of begetting life and of making it work. The same Spirit present at the Genesis creation, who brought life and order out of emptiness and chaos, is the One heaven still prescribes. The power that worked God's word

*G*OD THE CREATOR-FATHER CREATED, AND GOD THE HOLY SPIRIT TENDERLY ADMINISTERED THE MIGHTINESS NECESSARY TO ACCOMPLISH THE HUMANLY IMPOSSIBLE.

and will at the beginning of the created order, is the same power that brings God's word and will to pass in the redemptive order: The Holy Spirit. And He is the One announced power source to fulfill Christ's order in and through our lives today:

Receive the Holy Spirit....[and] you shall receive power when [He] has come upon you;...[that] the love of God has been poured out in our hearts...that you, being rooted and grounded in love, may be able to comprehend...Him who is able to do exceedingly abundantly above all that we ask or think, according to the power that works in us (John 20:22; Acts 1:8; Romans 5:5; Ephesians 3:17-20).

We should neither mystify nor muddy the two terms the angel uses in describing the Holy Spirit's new creation visitation of power available to come upon, and within, Mary. There is nothing mystical nor carnally suggestive. The frank words "come upon" and "overshadow" make two things clear in the Greek text, and they should be understood with equal simplicity and beauty in English. The plain language gives us the plain truth: God the Creator-Father *created*, and God the Holy Spirit tenderly *administered* the mightiness necessary to accomplish the humanly impossible.

This work of God's turning a hope into a reality is both gentle and pure. No explosive dynamo of laser beams is blazing with accompanying strobe lights. And it's certainly clear that nothing can possibly be construed as a supernatural experience of sexual intercourse. God's holy will working His holy purposes, and begetting His holy Son by the holy power of His Holy Spirit.

No sweat.

No suggestiveness.

But there was surrender.

This is a sensitive point in drawing our analogy. I want to be careful lest someone think me crude. But Mary's agreement was pivotal. She wasn't forced to accept her mission. The same truth applies to you and me. God seeks willing vessels who will *trust* Him and voluntarily open to Him. He will neither "seduce" us with deception nor "rape" our wills with sovereign power. In the Mary miracle we are shown that our surrender — in loving trust and resting faith — is needed.

The Necessary Response

After the angel explained to Mary how the conception could take place, she still needed to give her consent. And she did. It is expressed in her words, "Behold the maidservant of the Lord! Let it be to me according to your word."[1]

This is an important and discerning response, especially when we note Gabriel's earlier answer to her question. *Then,* the angel had said, "The Holy Spirit's *power* will accomplish this." But *now* Mary says, "Let the *word* you've spoken take effect."

There's a message here; it answers the common question: Which is most important or dynamic in God's kingdom order of operations: His Spirit or His Word.

The answer is yes: Yes to both!

We are to say "amen" to the proclamation of God's Word of truth and say "hallelujah" to the presence of His Spirit of power, and we are called to see them as equally essential, equally energizing, and to be certain they are equally embraced.

We don't have a videotaped recording of Mary's moment of conception, but we do have some tenderly warm and beautiful words—"come upon," "overshadow"—and both suggest *presence.* And we need offer no apology for the strong likelihood that the moment was emotion filled. However, with and alongside "presence" and "emotion," we discover *promise* and *reason.* We are given a very reasoned, logical explanation as to why the written promise is able to become a physical fact. Gabriel explains: "No word of God is without the inherent power to fulfill its intent." This is the more accurate translation of the words in Luke 1:27, "With God nothing will be impossible." The angels' declaration that the Spirit's power will be *present* is expanded with the explanation: *Within every promise of God are the life-giving, light-bearing seeds of mightiness needed to accomplish what God has said.*

Thus, the Mary miracle is worked with a balance: a *reason* is given to speak to the mind, and a *presence* is manifest that will inevitably stir the emotions. Because God created both—intellect and emotions—there is not only reason to believe both were quickened at this moment of encounter, but here is a compelling motive for us to open to and desire the quickening of our minds and emotions, too.

The Mary miracle not only invites us to believe God is ready to work wonders in and through us, but we are also shown exactly how that can be. We need to break free of doubt and fear—to open to the Word (dispelling doubt) and the Spirit (casting out fear). However dark or barren the womb of circumstance, there is a life power that God's Word *explains* to us, and there is a love power His Spirit is ready to *expand* in us. His truth and His grace are at hand. Now. But after all this is said, there is still something waiting to be done.

Surrender.

Submit to the terms of God's promise.

Submit to the moving of God's Spirit.

Remembering a Personal Struggle

I remember my own quest for the infilling (or

"baptism") of the Holy Spirit. It was during my college years, and my very collegiate mind was active with analytical questions about what God would do to me if I were to fully abandon my heart to the possibilities of a miraculous baptism—a divine visitation of God's Holy Spirit. There were real elements of a personal struggle involved.

My study of the New Testament warranted my belief that this encounter would be more than intellectually antiseptic—it might be "tainted" by my emotional involvement. (I certainly couldn't allow that!)

But having studied the experiences of various Bible personalities, I couldn't deny that praising, prophesying, tongue speaking, worshiping, rejoicing—all those responses—occurred in different situations. The allowance of emotion by these sensitive, sensible Bible personalities was obvious. Because I couldn't dismantle the biblical basis of these kinds of responses or manifestations, I finally gave in to God. I decided to do battle with my self-conscious fears. (And, along the way, I discovered and confessed that, for me, there was no small added issue of personal pride to be dealt with, too.)

Honesty was forcing me to come to terms with one fact: To allow God to have *full* control meant my risking the loss of *my* control. While I believed our Father never makes a fool out of anyone who runs that risk, I still felt cautious. But then, I remembered that Jesus promised safety in such surrender; and that satanic deception or self-delusion is impossible when full surrender is given to the Father—and in His presence.[2]

Our call is to yield ourselves to God—fully and without reserve, abandoned to His will and working in our lives. To encourage us, and to deepen a readiness to "let go and let God," let's take a look at some "surrender experiences" of key Bible characters:

> Abraham witnesses the fire of God's presence sweeping in upon his sacrifice as he surrenders to God's covenant (see Gen. 15).
>
> Moses is called to stand barefoot (an act of humility) as he is summoned to surrender to God's call at the burning bush (see Exod. 3).
>
> Samuel is told to talk back to the voice that calls him in the night, as he surrenders to His life-mission (see 1 Sam. 3).
>
> David unabashedly dances with a high display of joy, surrendering any pretension as he worships God (see 2 Sam. 6).

Isaiah sees the *shekinah* glory of God and cries out with conviction for sin as he surrenders to his prophetic call (see Isa. 6).

Peter is criticized and mocked as appearing intoxicated when he speaks with tongues, surrendering to the Spirit's infilling (see Acts 2).

Paul stumbles blindly, his pride and preconceptions overridden by God's power, bringing his surrender to the Savior's claims (see Acts 9).

John is prostrated in the presence of Christ; though an aged, seasoned saint, he isn't above a fresh surrender to his King (see Rev. 1).

The bottom line for me, as I sought the Holy Spirit infilling, was: There's no "neat" way to be open to the fullest moving of God's Spirit. To this day, it seems the best rule: If we want a Mary miracle, we have to be open to the Holy Spirit *coming upon* us, and the power of the highest *overshadowing* us.

"Coming upon" *(eperchomai)* literally bespeaks a greater power overcoming a weaker person, and is used in so simple a context as to describe sleep overtaking a wearied soul. "Overshadowed" *(episkiadzo)* reflects the spreading of wings, symbolizing the aboveness and mightiness of God, in whose superior shadow all humankind is left by comparison.

In short: We are invited to trust, and to lay ourselves open to God's mighty yet gentle power. I've never known "miracle grace" to be revealed from God's hand apart from the "loss of face" being granted by humans. The salvation of the human soul only ensues upon the human will to confess our sin and helplessness without God. Recovery only comes in the face of honesty; release, only in the wake of humility. The Mary miracle offers the pathway to God's wonder-workings—indeed! But the cost of opening to His power working in and through us is high: In Andrew Murray's words, it's *"Absolute surrender."*

Surrendering to His Power

My first visit to Nazareth occurred more than 25 years ago, when I investigated the site that seeks to preserve the likely location of the ancient home of Mary. While there, I was captivated by a deli-cately designed sculpture, a tasteful representa-tion of Mary at the moment of the conception.

Although I have frequently visited Israel for study tours, it was more than twenty years before I revisited that particular place. I returned later, however, especially because Anna had not been with me on that first trip, and I wanted her to see that statue.

When we arrived at the site, I was disappointed. The sculptured piece had been removed, our guide explained, "Because the priest said the people gave the statue too much attention." Upon closer inquiry, I learned it wasn't because they worshiped the figure, but because its unique warmth captivated them, as it had me, because of its humanness. (It apparently wasn't austere enough for the religious authorities.)

As I attempted to describe it to my wife, feeling sorry she would be unable to see it as I had years before, I was finding difficulty in knowing how to express what I had seen. Something about the piece breathed of a genuine trust—an openness to God. The artist had captured the spirit of Mary's "welcoming" the Holy Spirit to overshadow and work His miracle grace within her.

As I groped for words, I said, "Honey, it wasn't sexually suggestive, but the only way I can describe it is...she seemed to be saying..." I stopped, stymied for words.

But Anna finished the sentence: "She was saying, 'I'm Yours.'"

My eyes moistened and my heart warmed as Anna spoke those words. "Exactly," I answered, almost choking on the word as I felt the emotional impact of her womanly understanding.

For without cheapening what actually occurred as Mary fully opened herself to God's Spirit, my wife tenderly expressed what only a trusting, loving woman could understand. To surrender means to be open fully, purely and humbly, to love's presence; to present oneself without pretense or self-protection and say, "I'm yours, dear Lord."

And so it is for you and me to decide. The issue is without sexual inference or gender limit, but the Mary miracle awaits participants in its wonder possibilities today who will spread their arms in open welcome to the Spirit of God and embrace His fullest flow of love, life and miracle power.

To become pregnant with God's promise requires God's power—received with humility and accepted without reserve. Once you are open to that, you will find the Mary miracle "kind" of experience will do to you what a natural pregnancy does to anyone.

It will stretch you.

❧

PART 4

Learning
to Grow with
a Miracle

THEN MARY SAID, "BEHOLD THE MAIDSERVANT OF THE
LORD! LET IT BE TO ME ACCORDING TO YOUR WORD." AND
THE ANGEL DEPARTED FROM HER. ◆ NOW MARY AROSE IN
THOSE DAYS AND WENT INTO THE HILL COUNTRY WITH
HASTE, TO A CITY OF JUDAH, AND ENTERED THE HOUSE OF
ZACHARIAS AND GREETED ELIZABETH. —LUKE 1:38-40

Miracles aren't as welcome in this world as we
might hope or think. When you receive one, you
will likely find it more demanding to carry, deliver
and live with than it was to conceive at its inception.

AND IT HAPPENED, WHEN ELIZABETH HEARD THE GREETING OF MARY, THAT THE BABE LEAPED IN HER WOMB; AND ELIZABETH WAS FILLED WITH THE HOLY SPIRIT.

THEN SHE SPOKE OUT WITH A LOUD VOICE AND SAID, "BLESSED ARE YOU AMONG WOMEN, AND BLESSED IS THE FRUIT OF YOUR WOMB!

"BUT WHY IS THIS GRANTED TO ME, THAT THE MOTHER OF MY LORD SHOULD COME TO ME?

"FOR INDEED, AS SOON AS THE VOICE OF YOUR GREETING SOUNDED IN MY EARS, THE BABE LEAPED IN MY WOMB FOR JOY.

"BLESSED IS SHE WHO BELIEVED, FOR THERE WILL BE A FULFILLMENT OF THOSE THINGS WHICH WERE TOLD HER FROM THE LORD."

AND MARY SAID:

"MY SOUL MAGNIFIES THE LORD,

AND MY SPIRIT HAS REJOICED IN GOD MY SAVIOR.

FOR HE HAS REGARDED THE LOWLY STATE OF HIS MAIDSERVANT;

FOR BEHOLD, HENCEFORTH ALL GENERATIONS WILL CALL ME BLESSED.

FOR HE WHO IS MIGHTY HAS DONE GREAT THINGS FOR ME, AND HOLY IS HIS NAME."

LUKE 1:41-49

CHAPTER TEN

Having a Baby Will Stretch You

The chill of the Indiana springtime night still hung lightly in the air as I briskly walked toward the car. The signs of dawn were in the eastern sky, although the sun was probably an hour from fully rising.

It was Easter morning.

Anna was resting now. Fourteen hours of labor were behind her, and our first child, a baby girl, was in the hospital nursery on the third floor of the building.

If I get to bed right away, I might get three hours sleep before having to rise for church, I thought to myself. *The people are going to be ecstatic.*

I know I was! Rebecca Lynn Hayford had been ushered into this world only an hour before, and now we were a full-blown family. My excitement was so immediate and rich, the small "glitch" in Anna's birthing process didn't seem to make any difference.

A Physical Change

Something had torn during the delivery.

It's an indelible memory. The doctor was so earnestly concerned that I clearly understand, that his tone in describing what had happened scared me at first.

"Mr. Hayford, there's something I have to tell you about your wife's physical condition."

He wasn't urgent, but the words by themselves seemed ominous, and what was probably a kind of apology that things weren't perfect, came out with something of a hint of the tragic. Though we had just finished with the smiles and congratulations while I had studied the baby's tiny form only minutes before, he had my full attention. He must have caught my worried look, because he immediately took a less threatening tack.

"There isn't any real need to be concerned, Jack. Anna's all right. But I want you to understand something that happened to her. It isn't uncommon, but it is not normally repairable.

"A major abdominal muscle has torn, and it means there will now be certain limits to how fully her normal shape will be able to resume itself. It won't be unsightly, but it will certainly be noticeable. I'm sorry; it's simply the cost sometimes of carrying and delivering a child."

I asked questions aimed at assuring myself that nothing was serious about the situation. When I finally was certain that aesthetics were all that was involved, I took comfort.

Even then, neither Anna nor I had any illusions about life not taking some toll on our bodies. (For example, I had already begun balding and wasn't nervous about it.) At twenty-something, living and aging were no threats, nor have they ever been as years have accumulated. But the episode comes to mind as we discuss the Mary miracle because, just as with my wife, so is it with us all: Having a baby will stretch you.

The Bible doesn't mention whether Mary had morning sickness, how many stretch marks (striae, they're called) remained on her body or how long labor was for her delivery of the world's Savior. But these facts of life travel right along with the fundamentals that explain "where babies come from."

Though Mary's came from a different source

than any other infant in history, the physical costs
and inconveniences, along with discomforts and
nausea that attend most normal pregnancies,
would have been hers as well.

They will probably be ours, too.

Counting the Cost

Just as Mary's faith was stretched to conceive,
her body was stretched to carry and deliver. The
analogy of the Mary miracle has a good deal to
say to and inquire of us at these points, too. Let
me phrase a few questions:

1. Are you willing to trade in your "trim,
girlish figure" for a "slightly used" body?

By that, of course, I mean to note that being
open to the Mary miracle can change the shape of
your life, especially in the eyes of others. If I am
preoccupied with appearances and too concerned
about how people see me, it is possible I might
renege on God's offer to work wonders through
me.

Just as some women opt against pregnancy
because they are unwilling to risk the beauty of
their own bodies in order to bear the life and
growth of another, so it is with some saints. The

thought of being seen with spiritual stretch marks seems grotesque.

These striae often can come, for example, by reason of a person's receiving a new dimensioned fullness of the "new wine" Jesus offers. To people too tightly wrapped in the security of familiar systems, Jesus said drinking His wine is risky. If it can explode old wineskins, we can be sure it will certainly stretch even the most flexible believer.

Inevitably, the expanding work of the Holy Spirit—with new power bringing new life—can and will change your shape forever!

> 2. Are you willing to live with the fact that pregnancy will dramatically change the way you walk?

We are all aware that a growing fetus swells the tummy area, and we have seen how the body's added pounds and different weight distribution creates a new center of gravity. In later months, a pregnant woman is likely to waddle more than walk, often slightly rolling from side to side, rather than exhibiting a more poised stride. It is a part of the process—accepted, maybe smiled at, and admired occasionally—but it is a gait that is definitely different.

One of my newest friends in public ministry is

a man whose life has been drastically affected by the fact that God has begun to move in regular displays of miracle mightiness through him. It has been an awkward load for him to carry, especially because some onlookers are disturbed by the different walk to which God has called him.

Critics chide or mock, notwithstanding the inescapable authenticity of many miracles. They seem oblivious or indifferent to the fact that, because my friend was open to this "pregnancy," hundreds of sick and afflicted people have been healed, delivered or brought to Christ.

People are often preoccupied and more concerned with social poise than with spiritual power.

Now, your or my experience with the Mary miracle might not involve so widely visible or vulnerable a point of noticeable difference in our walk as my friend's has. But count on this, dear one. Once you allow God to work new dimensions of Christ's life in you by the Holy Spirit's power, it will affect how you live—both in human eyes as well as God's.

- Our walk with Him will become more dependent.
- Our walk before friends and associates will become more noticeably "His walk."
- Our walk before a watching world will

become more frequently evaluated by others, stressing the need to show ourselves reliable and purposeful.

These changes aren't to be pretensions of piety, forced by a sudden sense of need to appear religious. Instead (and, thankfully, this is so true), these traits of change can arrive and develop with a natural and desirable quality—something that will cause normal, noncritical onlookers to respond in positive terms.

You have heard people say it: "A woman is never more beautiful than when she's pregnant." Whether it's always true in the biological realm or not, God's Spirit can make it true of you and me in our spiritual walk, expanding with the Mary miracle. We might seem different, but we might also become beautiful.

A New Diet?

3. Are you willing to accept a new, disciplined diet and pattern of refusing self-indulgence, since you are now being open to live your life for more than only yourself?

Posters warn, doctors counsel and wise women

listen: When pregnant, certain substances need to absolutely be avoided, and dietary precautions need to be carefully observed.

THE STEP TOWARD SPIRITUAL ADULTHOOD THAT IS CHARACTERIZED BY ONE'S DECISION TO BE OPEN TO THE MARY MIRACLE CALLS FOR AN END TO CHILDISH, PERSONAL INDULGENCES.

There's no need to elaborate the obvious because the analogy is probably clear enough to you already. Once I commit to the Holy Spirit's coming to work His larger grace and increased glory in my life, I'm mistaken if I think what I ingest won't make any difference.

My intake—through my social life, my enter-
tainment interests, my personal habits or even my
allowances in conversation content—will all need
a movement toward maturity. Paul said, "When I
became a man, I put away childish things" (1 Cor.
13:11). The step toward spiritual adulthood that
is characterized by one's decision to be open to
the Mary miracle calls for an end to childish, personal indulgences.

But be cautioned, and also discerning.

There is, and has been, a tradition of "list creating" at certain times and places in past, and current, church life. Such lists usually indicate ritual
rules or sets of requirements that a given group
expects of their constituents in order to verify a
member's "holiness." Thereby, the person's
acceptability in the congregation or allowability
to lead is determined. In fact, a person's ability to
expect God's blessing is often tied to such sched-
ules of performance.

But the new walk I'm discussing isn't born of
such external pressure. Instead, it derives from
something—no, *Someone*—growing His life and
wonders inside you, and we're never expected to
affect a walk, only to accept it with sensitivity and
graciousness.

Inevitably, lists become counterproductive.
They often introduce a disappointing pride in

those who meet their peers' demands, and frequently tend to prompt rebellion in those rejected for their imperfection. True practical holiness can't be legislated, but at the same time it should be longed for.

So, let all "pregnant saints" be discerning. The call to a wonderwalk with the Lord is no lightweight proposition. For the weight of the glory He begins to work within us as we are open to His Spirit deserves to be honored for its true worth.

As a baby within the womb calls for a judicious sensitivity to purity, discipline and self-denial, so a miracle-in-process within recommends the same. Miracles aren't the product of our commitment to a more worthy walk with God, because our worthiness is not what begets the potential of His wonders. But recklessness can ruin or abort a Mary miracle in progress. Tragedies in recent high-profile ministries are sad, but eloquent, illustrations of this.

Walk softly, dear one. His life within, designed to multiply and bless many besides yourself, is not fragile—but it is precious. Treat it that way.

We can learn a lot between Nazareth and Bethlehem.

CHAPTER ELEVEN

When You're All Alone Again

There's an oft-unnoticed candor in the statement, "And the angel departed from her" (Luke 1:38). What is probably most often casually passed over as an unimportant, transitional footnote to the essential features of the story is actually an observation of a critical fact: Miracles conceived at high moments of faith still have to be carried through long seasons of waiting.

A Time of Questions and Doubts

First, be assured that the angel's departure wasn't an act of forsaking Mary. But it certainly must have set the scene for some lonely self-questioning.

I propose that Mary wondered things such as the following because all of us who have ever tasted even the slightest sweetness of God's promises being begotten in us have wondered similar things. Once the angel is gone, when you are all alone again, thoughts such as the following are inevitable:

> *Did I actually hear what I think I heard? Or have I somehow talked myself into the belief that God is going to do something great in and through me?*
>
> *If I'm really a loved and chosen person who is open to becoming an avenue of God's grace and life-begetting blessing, why do I feel so unsupernatural now, and so alone?*
>
> *What's going to happen now? I was open to something wonderful, and did experience a genuinely wonderful beginning. But nothing wonderful is happening that I can see—not right here, or right now.*

Have you ever wondered what Mary's reaction was to the first sign she received, revealing that the miracle she was promised was actually happening—growing within her?

From the most basic point of human observation, we all know this: Her first sign would have been *no sign at all.*

It may seem either too mundane to mention, or I might strike someone as making a too-human-to-observe comment, or possibly even a tasteless one. But Mary's first sign would have been when her monthly cycle failed to arrive at its usual time; that is, "no sign at all."

That obvious observation should provide no surprise to us and what it suggests shouldn't either. Because when the promise of any miracle is received and genuinely set in motion, the most common thing to happen is nothing—or less than nothing.

You received Christ at a church or group gathering, but the next day at home the absence of affirming people and the waning of emotion prompt a wondering. Did God really notice? Can this really be true—me? Forgiven completely? Saved forever? That signless morning after has even tougher ramifications at times.

- You are open to God's promise that your marriage can be healed and your relationship can become strong, and a fierce argument erupts between you.
- You receive a stir of faith that persuades you with the certainty that your wayward

child will be reclaimed, and he goes on a bender with drugs.

- You see a beautiful breakthrough in the worship life of your congregation, promising real revival, then a visitor interrupts your Sunday morning gathering with a fanatical display that sets the congregation back to its earlier reserve, disallowing warmth and expectancy.

This order of "the first sign is no sign at all"—or worse, the disappearance of what hopeful signs you ever had—may well have been a struggle for Mary, too.

Consider this: Is it possible that missing her regular cycle didn't assure Mary? Is it possible that instead of thinking, *Praise God, this proves the miracle is happening,* she might have been tempted to think something else?

Might she have thought, *Maybe this whole thing is something I've simply convinced myself of. How long has it been? Two weeks since I thought I talked with that angel? And where is he since then, anyway?*

Is it possible she could remember conversations with her mother, her sisters or other women—ladies who knew that sometimes overexcitement can delay or interrupt a woman's pattern of menstruation?

Maybe that's it. I'm just worked up, excited, with no real reason to be, other than my own overactive imagination! (Incidentally, where are angels when you really need them?)

Let's not think it less than faithlike or saintly that Mary might have felt such feelings or thought such questions.

It is an outright shame that the fallacy has ever been taught that people who have doubts can't please God. That lying argument evolves from such texts as, "Whatever is not from faith is sin" (Rom. 14:23) and "For let not that man suppose that he will receive anything from the Lord; he is a double-minded man, unstable in all his ways" (Jas. 1:7,8).

But that's not the *whole* truth. Remember also: Sarah laughed with semiskeptical wonder, and still conceived the miracle of Isaac. Gideon challenged, "I've never seen miracles in my time," and God gave him wondrous victory. Peter sank in Galilee's waters, distracted by doubt, but was lifted to walk in a wonder again.

Clearly, neither of the previous two texts, nor any others in God's Word, dismiss any of us from miracle possibilities simply because we are tempted with doubt or questions. It is one thing to wrestle with doubts and another thing to submit to them, one thing to struggle with questions and another to answer them with human reasonings rather than God's Word.

Wherever miracle possibilities are offered by God, never forget this: Since it is His sovereign grace that has made the promise, it will be His omnipotent power that is going to fulfill it.

We are the privileged vessels for such glorious workings, and our openness is essential to their occurring. But we are neither the originators nor the finishers of such wonders. We are simply His beloved ones, who have chosen to surrender to His desire to work wonderfully in and through us.

Mary didn't become the fulfillment of Isaiah 7:14 by repeating the promise over and over until she became convinced she had adequately claimed it for herself. ("A virgin shall conceive....A virgin shall conceive....A virgin shall conceive....Praise God, I believe that's for me!")

But, on the other hand, let's make no mistake: Mary *did* choose to receive that word when God Himself offered it to her. She *did* surrender herself to the Holy Spirit, who was present to initiate the power flow of holy grace that would eventually bring that word to fulfillment.

Still, those commitments don't dehumanize anyone. The whole of the Bible's narrative about Mary reveals her vulnerability to doubt's temptation at other times. There's no reason to feel it demeans the sweet woman or her miracle to think she "wondered" about it herself.

And nothing in the Bible requires you or me to become mechanical spouters of Scripture to have God's Word fulfilled in our lives.

- Yes, we should declare God's promises!
- Yes, we should address doubt with God's Word!
- Yes, we should refuse to counter with our lips what God's Spirit has revealed in the Scriptures and quickened to our hearts!

But never—*never*—become hopeless, condemned or defeated because doubt lifts its head or questions come to your mind. When you are carrying a miracle, there are times little or nothing is happening to verify your pregnancy. Or something may seem about to abort it.

Seasons of Dilemma

I experienced this dilemma a few years ago when a marvelous property was made available for acquisition by our congregation. Our cramped situation and our burgeoning ministry possibilities logically recommended we move toward the purchase—a challenging one involving several millions of dollars.

Though I had not told the congregation before this, nearly 10 years earlier the Holy Spirit had put it in my heart: I was to ask for that property, believe we would someday own it, but tell no one about it. Now the offer was real and action was being taken at the direction of our congregation's board. They were acting completely without any constraint because of my "word from the Lord," for I had not told them about that.

Soon, the property went into escrow. We were on our way to realizing the closing of the deal, and I was rejoicing in the imminent fulfillment of what I had been open to receive and believe... *then*! Then the deal fell out of escrow.

Drastic changes in the whole circumstance presented themselves. Our board had no choice but to withdraw, and so the door slammed shut. The miracle baby seemed to be dead in the womb!

I was totally bewildered.

After all, God had spoken to me; I had been open to Him in faith; He had mightily confirmed His word; an entire congregation had been moving toward the realization of a miracle provision. Then...crash!

I was suddenly faced with one of the most demanding circumstances of my entire ministry.

Although I had made no public claim that "God told me we'd have this property," it certainly did appear His will was that we would. Furthermore, within my heart, I *did* know that He had spoken to me.

At least I had thought so, until now.

That's when the temptation to doubt arose and a proliferation of inner questions went on a field day, marching and stomping through my mind.

What happened, Lord? Did I really hear from you? Was I only talking myself into something? Am I nothing more than a gullible, self-convincing goof? Was there something wrong that I did? Have I moved in blind, arrogant presumption? Were we on track with faith, and now I've somehow gotten off track and violated faith?

The seemingly unlimited capacity of the mind to badger you and the untiring efforts of the adversary to accuse or condemn you seem to multiply such seasons of dilemma. But amid all this I made a decision. It involved three things:

1. I needed to "lay down" the property at Jesus' feet and be unafraid of anything that happened. It was to be His to have or release, as I put it under His control and removed it entirely from the clutch of my concerned, "hope-for" fingers.

2. I would not attempt to "explain God" to

anyone. Realizing that since I actually didn't know why things had seemingly been snatched from us when we thought

Living with a miracle means far more than experiencing its conception. It means resting in God's promise and power even when it seems the miracle isn't going to be born.

※

them firmly in hand, I would not pretend to know or to interpret God's apparent change of mind for us. Though it's often hard (especially for spiritual leaders) to admit our lack of omniscience, it's gloriously freeing when we do.

3. I would pray for the property every time
   I drove past it, which was almost every
   day. My prayer was not an action of insis-
   tence, as though I felt my prayer was a
   means I was to employ to wrest the matter back from some power who had seized
   it from us. Rather, my prayer was a confession of faith: "Lord, I simply trust *You*,
   and I simply keep that property in Your
   hands, to do with as You will."

I actually felt no gripping conviction of anything else than a peace that God was almighty
and the matter was His. I will not say I "believed
we would receive it." I *did* believe God had earlier impressed on me that it would be ours, but now
I didn't know why it wasn't happening, or if it
ever would.

So I chose to simply praise Him. After all, I was
sure He Himself was far more important than anything we would ever receive or believe anyway!

It's too long a story to relate how the reversal
came about, but about ten weeks later—*with no
promise whatsoever of a resurrecting possibility being
present*—the door that had slammed closed suddenly reopened. We did nothing to force it and
were amazed when it did, so when the reversal
occurred, two things happened:

- Everyone could clearly see this was most certainly something of God's will and design.
- God received the glory entirely (and a miracle cash flow began that amazingly expedited the acquisition).

Living with a Miracle in the Womb

Living with a miracle means far more than experiencing its conception. It means resting in God's promise and power even when it seems the miracle isn't going to be born. It means believing you really did hear God's word to you, even "after the angel has departed."

Living with a miracle still in the womb, as yet not manifest to anyone other than you, calls for a point of understanding greater than knowing God's works and workings: simply knowing *Him*. Far beyond His power, He wants you to know His person.

- Knowing the truth of His Word, mastering it by the sincerest study, doesn't attain this knowledge.
- Entering into the mightiest experiences of His Spirit's gifts and power doesn't achieve this intimacy.

Whatever wonders the Mary miracle is designed to introduce to, in and through our lives, these are not the primary objectives. The ultimate wonder is knowing intimately and increasingly the Wonder-worker. My whole experience with the apparent failure of a project, and my questions whether I had heard God or not, were reinforcements of this principle.

God's greatest goal with any of us is to have *us*. His mightiness is not offered to make impressive displays through us (though He's willing to avenue His grace through human vessels). And His power has never been promised in order to entertain human fancies by manifesting the miraculous for exhibition or excitement (though His workings are stunning).

Never.

Rather, we come to learn that God wants to work wonders because He is "wonder-full." And more than anything else, He wants us to know *Him*, to desire His presence more than His power, and to seek His face fully, more than hoping to see His "force-fullness."

When a Mary miracle "kind" of thing begins in any of us, surely the time will come when we feel we are all alone again; a time when the Spirit's presence, warmth and truth, which quickened the promise of God's Word to our spirits, now seems long past—even subject to doubt.

But there's a sure remedy for that "aloneness" because there's a changeless certainty. Now, as with Mary, the fact stands unshakable. Whatever else happens, you are not alone. The promise is still true. And His power is at work within you.

Take these three facts and let them move you from expecting a wonder to embracing Him who is wonderful. His angel may have departed, but He is always right there.

All the way until His baby is born. And beyond.

❧

CHAPTER TWELVE

On the "Mary Way" to Handling Miracles

Contrary to popular belief, miracles don't happen instantaneously. They may *ignite* in a moment, and even *excite* at their inception, but let's get it right: Miracles take a long time. And they call forth a mind-set that not only believes for a miracle but that will also learn to walk in it.

We may indeed open to the *beginning* of faith's acceptance, through full surrender. But as time passes, and it seems things are moving slowly, if at all, questions and doubts sometimes seem relentless in their quest to remove our "expectation." So between Nazareth and Bethlehem, we may need counsel as to the ways to behave in *keeping* the spirit of surrender, faith and submission to the promise as we wait. Because, *yes*—miracles do take time.

Dealing with Delays and Liabilities

How many hours, for example, do you suppose it took to walk through the Red Sea when it opened? And how much faith do you think it took for the last of the multitude to step forward, as compared to the first ones? (Can you imagine someone saying, "I wonder just how long those waves can stay piled up that way?")

Whatever joy Mary experienced in receiving the beginning of her miracle, we would be careless if we overlooked the time it would take or the liabilities she incurred. Just to summarize a few:

- She has a nine-month pregnancy to carry unto delivery.
- There's the problem of "How do I tell Joseph?"
- What will the two of them say to those who are skeptical about the time discrepancy between their marriage and the baby's birth?

And then, there are liabilities she couldn't foresee:

- Where to find a "delivery room" when you're in a town with no space left for travelers.
- What to say when shepherds "fresh from the field" crowd around and you've just had a baby.
- How to chart an escape route from a murderous king.

And you'll appreciate this (especially if you've traveled there):

- How can you nourish a healthy baby when you both have to drink the water in Egypt!!

We might smile at some of these liabilities, but whether serious or facetious, they remind us that a miracle initiated in a moment sets a path toward a whole new realm of responsibilities as well as possibilities.

And there's a "Mary way" to respond.

Mary illustrates at least three primary lessons, ways that you and I would be wise to note and apply. Once we open ourselves to God's grace and power working something new and wonderful in us, these principles can help us carry our miracle—"full term, unto delivery"—as well as care for the wonderful thing God gives us.

Serve Someone Else's Miracle

Lesson One: The Mary way to respond to a miracle promise begun in your life is to find how you can serve the miracle God is working in someone else.

Mary's trip to Elizabeth's house can be interpreted in either of two ways—or the combination of both. We don't know if she was hoping simply to get out of town for a while, *until I figure all of this out;* or if she was thinking, *I'd better go spend some time with my older cousin Elizabeth; being pregnant at her age, she could use a friend's help!* It's more than likely that both these issues factored into her decision.

As we earlier examined what happened when she first arrived at Elizabeth's house, it's clear that God's purpose in Mary's trip was as much for her benefit as for Elizabeth's. But there's a lot to be said for the "heart" she manifests in going to her cousin. The angel gives no specific command that

Mary go and assist Elizabeth but only mentions that she is carrying a child, too.

The Bible says that Mary stayed there for nearly three months until Elizabeth's baby was born. The immediacy of her going to help, and the duration of her time spent at Elizabeth's—right up to John's birth—provide us with an insight into Mary's character. She was at least as ready to serve another person's miracle as she was to welcome her own. It's not hard to imagine a multitude of ways the younger woman would have worked around the house, gone to the well for water, shopped at the market. Her cousin was quite aged,[1] and was advanced in the term of her pregnancy. So who can measure what Mary's diligence and loving service may have meant to her senior-in-years cousin in assuring the success of Elizabeth's pregnancy.

We have no record of anything more than a few words—"three months"—but it isn't difficult to imagine something of the private conversations that would have taken place between the two women.

Mary and Elizabeth were both recipients of unusual and wonderful pregnancies—vastly different, yet very much alike. But Elizabeth's had begun first, and she was also an older woman with more experience with life. We may do well to contemplate Mary's benefit from, as well as service to, Elizabeth, for nothing has helped me more through the years than the privilege of learning from people whose "miracle" is farther along than mine.

Spending time with those who have walked the way of faith before you—even if you, like Mary, have the advantage of greater position or privilege—is essential to any of our growth in wisdom. I learned something of this truth a few years ago.

When God began to so vastly expand the congregation I pastor—performing "the great work" He had promised—sometime afterward I decided to make two special requests. At separate times, I invited two men, both a full generation older than I was, to come and help me.

Dr. Vincent Bird and Rev. Maurice Tolle were each headed into retirement. What we might call the "miracle years" of their more active ministry, were yielding way to those harvest years that await faith-filled seniors who know that God is never through working His wonders in and through our lives.

Vincent was my first bishop, and Maurice was the pastor who preached the night I received Christ as a ten-year-old boy. Both of these men were like fathers to me, and both had preceded me for decades in the demanding task of pastoral ministry.

My first concern was to show my care for them; rendering respect for their service to God's kingdom, as well as thanksgiving for the blessing they had been to me. Then, inviting them to a part-time retirement position was an opportunity to provide a further meaningful use of their gifts. On the one hand, we were allowed to contribute to their support, to assure they were cared for as their later years increased; on the other, I profited from their prayer partnership, their fruitful service and their just plain "being there."

More than anything we might have been able to provide for them—I was interested in drawing on the experience, wisdom and counsel they could give me. Although neither of them had ever pastored a church larger than five hundred members (and by reason of God's "great work," I was serving one with more than five thousand), I knew that wisdom is not measured by human quantitative systems. Mary's miracle turned out to be more far-reaching in impact than Elizabeth's, but Mary clearly knew the value of a senior's partnership, as well as the rightness of serving their need.

Like Mary, I needed the prophetic encouragement and comforting partnership of someone more mature, who had been living with a miracle longer than I had. Maurice blessed me right up to his recent homegoing this year, at age eighty-five, while "Doc Bird," as we affectionately call him, is still a constant reservoir of care and support at age eighty-two.

The "Mary way" works; I can attest to it. Yes, what Mary was experiencing was far and away larger than what Elizabeth had received: The Messiah exceeds His forerunner. But in serving her "senior-in-miracle-grace," Mary points the way for you and me. Serving someone else's miracle will not only nourish your faith with strength to carry your own, but I can assure you: You'll gain comfort and wisdom beyond anything you could ever accrue singlehandedly.

Sing to the Lord

Lesson Two: Receive a song to sing: It's the Holy Spirit's way to cultivate the joy of the Lord, and that's a secret to regenerating our spiritual strength — day to day.

A dozen themes are contained in the song Mary sings in Luke 1:46-55: themes of joy, humility, victory, trial, promise and so on. They all have a time and place for our appropriation. We will need each one at one point or another as we enter and pursue our walk with God into, and toward, His miracle purposes in our lives.

Mary's song deserves our close examination, but I am not going to do it for you. Instead, just as you have opened to receive the beginning of God's good grace doing new wonders in you, allow time to sit down alone with Luke 1:46-55, to meditate over the verses as you take them phrase by phrase. Above all, notice the confidence-inspiring words that repeatedly focus on the great, central fact: *"God is the source of my miracle!"* Let your heart be constantly steadied by that truth, and learn to *sing* it.

Carrying any miracle to birth will bring the soul through seasons of weariness, of discomfort, of criticism, of vulnerability to depression and more. These are all common syndromes of a normal physical pregnancy; so don't be surprised at the parallel in your Mary miracle "kind" of experience. But whenever your "wonder walk" seems to become something less than wonderful, when strained, stressed or discouraged by reason of life's simplest realities or its most difficult attacks, the "Mary way" to handle such times is to sing!

• Have a hymnal on hand and review the

lyrics (even memorize some), for the most durable hymns are those that have power to speak God's promise and hope into the most trying times people have faced.

- Read from the Book of Psalms, *every day*. The full gamut of human emotions—from ecstasy to anguish—is expressed here. And they dynamically renew hope in the confidence that the Lord's presence will abide with us. The conclusion regularly drawn is that "through it all" God will be there unfailingly, and "beyond it all" you will triumph.

- Let music fill your ears, whether in your home or in your car. Sustain an atmosphere of strengthening joy by playing collections of praise music. And sing along! Even if you don't feel like it, or doubt your talent—sing. "Again I say, Rejoice" (Phil. 4:4, *KJV*).

- Write your own song. It doesn't need to be rhythmically, lyrically or musically perfect—nor even be shared with anyone. But sing your feelings of thanks to God, "singing with grace in your hearts to the Lord" (Col. 3:16).

There's a power-filled fact in that last text.

Paul taught the Colossians that God's word incarnates itself "richly"—that is, profitably and increasingly—as we join our song to His promise. So do it! As Mary did, let your song become a practical means for sustaining the joy and strength of the Lord until your miracle comes to its time of delivery.

Keep Simple of Soul

Lesson Three: Be free from any pressure to know everything or to explain anything. Simply let the One who has begun the miracle in you, process it by His power and for His glory.

A charming simplicity continually flows from the Gospel narrative where Mary is involved. She simply lets God do what He is able to do, and as the miracle in her moves forward, the Lord takes full care of His purposed work in her, without Mary's need for explanations or self-defense. We see this later in the story:

- In the way the Lord reveals to Joseph the holy source of her pregnancy, relieving Mary of the need to persuade him or protect herself. (So you can let God convince others of what He is doing in you; don't accept the burden of becoming self-verifying or self-defensive.)

*M*ARY MIRACLES ARE A KIND OF THING GOD WANTS TO DO IN MULTITUDES OF PEOPLE IN ORDER TO TRANSFORM A WORLD OF NEED-FILLED CIRCUMSTANCES. AND YOU AND I ARE PRIVILEGED TO DECLARE CANDIDACY FOR SUCH GRACES IF WE ARE WILLING TO BE OPEN TO HIM ON HIS TERMS.

❧

- In the way she responds when the shepherds come with the report of angels. Mary doesn't smugly tell them, "I knew it already," as though to assert her superior role or knowledge. She simply "kept all these things and pondered them in her heart" (Luke 2:19). (So we are wise to learn to keep still amid God's wonder-graces, and not fall into the trap of pretension or self-importance.)

There is a right way to carry a miracle, a way that keeps God's glory untainted by any claim on a person's part to be even slightly responsible for it. Mary's humble and homely wisdom deserves our remembrance as well as our review. If we accept a pregnancy in God's purpose for our lives, we'll need to remember the way to carry it.

Mary miracles are a "kind" of thing God wants to do in multitudes of people in order to transform a world of need-filled circumstances. And you and I are privileged to declare candidacy for such graces if we are willing to be open to Him on His terms.

But when we do, let's remember the Mary way to carry the miracle, too. Learn to *serve, sing* and keep *simple of soul.*

And in conclusion, may I ask you one thing more. Let me ask you to do something, having the sum of these several lessons in your heart.

Please answer the phone.

CHAPTER THIRTEEN

*Someone Is
on the Phone*

Raissa was discouraged if not desperate.

After more than three years of marriage, she had not been able to conceive, and her deep desire to have a baby was becoming an even deeper frustration.

She and Don had invited the prayer of friends on many occasions. Then, one Sunday after church, she came to me to ask for special prayer.

Prayer Brought a Healing

In many situations, the elders of our congregation have been requested to pray for couples who have not been able to have children. Often, as in

Raissa's case, physiological problems are present, and the prayer is more for a healing than it is for pregnancy.

We have never claimed we "have a gift" for praying babies into being. But in a rather remarkable number of instances, apparent infertility, or some other difficulty, has been overcome by the grace of God through answered prayer. So that day she asked, I placed my hand on Raissa's head and prayed for her in Jesus' name, "Lord, fulfill the desire of this woman's heart."

At the time, I didn't know her precise problem. Later, however, I learned that her doctor had diagnosed a blockage in both fallopian tubes that, short of a surgical procedure, would disable her from ever having a child.

Don was a seminary student finishing his studies for entry into the Presbyterian ministry, and he and Raissa had been attending our church for more than two years. So given the much smaller size of our congregation at that time, it wasn't difficult to schedule the luncheon Raissa hosted and to which they invited Anna and me several weeks later.

In the meantime, following my prayer for her, Raissa had written to me: "Pastor Jack," the note said, "when you finished praying for me, you very specifically said, 'You are going to have a baby.'

I'm writing to simply ask: Did you say that only to be comforting to me, or did you say that because you felt the Lord prompted you to?"

I wasn't offended by her inquiry, for the young woman had a tender heart and a sweet spirit. I understood and, immediately upon receiving her letter, turned to my desk to handwrite a note in return.

I expressed myself on the basis of the Holy Spirit's firm prompting at the time we had prayed. It was easy to assure her that I wasn't inventing a feeling or toying with a humanistically generated idea. She and Don's involvement in our church family had already taught them that we don't dabble in such guesswork.

But still, she was one very anxious girl, longing desperately to become a mother, and she was "checking" at every turn. I wrote, "No, Raissa, I wasn't 'simply being comforting,' but I do believe the promises of God's Word hold a power that is for you as well as many others."

A Divinely Appointed Phone Call?

Now the luncheon day had come.

Anna and I had arrived shortly after noon at this loving couple's little apartment in Pasadena, near the seminary. The room was bright and airy, the curtains blowing slightly in the early afternoon breeze, which the open windows allowed us all to enjoy. In just a few minutes, we were at the simply, but beautifully, set table, as Raissa had graciously arranged to fit the lunchtime to our very tight schedule.

Quite soon, the conversation moved to the matter that was constantly on our hostess's mind. She had no unpleasantness in her tone, only an earnest longing—one shared by Don as well.

While we were discussing our exchange of letters, the phone rang. Don, being nearest, lifted the receiver and answered. What followed has become one of the most memorable moments in the lives of both the couples at that lunch.

Don's face looked puzzled at what was being said on the other end of the line; then he answered: "No, this isn't your daddy," he said gently. "I think you have the wrong number."

He hung up and, with a strange, questioning look on his face, explained: "It was a little boy, who only said, 'Is this my daddy?'"

Exactly as he spoke those words, a pulse of the Holy Spirit's presence flushed over my soul. I felt compelled to say something I sensed He was strongly impressing upon my heart and mind.

"Don and Raissa, you know I'm not a fanatic.

But I have to tell you what the Lord is giving me right now."

A MIRACLE IS ANY INVASION OF EARTH WITH THE WORKINGS AND GRACE OF HEAVEN'S POWER, LOVE AND LIFE. THESE MIRACLES ARE WAITING IN THE WINGS, SOME OF THEM PERHAPS BEING ANNOUNCED THROUGH THIS SMALL BOOK AS THE HOLY SPIRIT MAY USE IT TO SPEAK. PERHAPS TO YOU. PERHAPS NOW.

❧

You could feel the presence of God in the room. All four of us perceived an unusual moment was being experienced together. In the middle of a rather everyday conversation, it seemed the love of God had stepped in to make an announcement.

"I'm sure," I continued, "that whoever that little boy was, he did have the wrong number—humanly speaking. But the Lord wants you to know that *He* arranged the call getting to you—because He is saying, 'Don, you *are* a daddy! Raissa, you *will* have a baby!'"

The confirming sense of the Lord's nearness was so close that none of us needed to explain our readiness to believe to the other. We were and are—none of us—gullible creatures. But the God of all life and love had pervaded the setting in such a way that we all knew He had spoken to us, and we were drawn to prayerful praise about the sense of certainty we felt regarding His promise to "make the barren to sing" (see Isa. 54:1).

Two weeks later the doctor declared Raissa pregnant!

In fact, that's when she learned she had already conceived—prior to the lunchtime Anna and I spent with them. Don was already a daddy when the call came!

When they both met me at church a few days after her appointment with the obstetrician, we had one wonderful time of laughter over the special, custom-made ways of our precious Lord.

None of us had any superstitious notions that the call was from a little voice in heaven, giving advance notice. But *some* little boy's fingers did fumble a number by divine appointment—I'm sure of it. And two hearts leaped at a promise that day, while two more rejoiced in faith. And two things more:

Their baby was a boy.

And they named him Isaac.

It's a Kind of Prophecy

I wanted to save Raissa and Don's story for the end of this book. It's a great story, because it holds so many elements of the very things we have been talking about:

- People *do* feel longings that seem unanswered.
- People *do* become desperate, discouraged or frustrated.
- Problems *do* produce real blockages to possibilities.
- Prayers *are* made but seem so long in being answered.
- God *does* speak, and calls us to believe He means it.

- Signs *are* given, though sometimes strange and wonderful.
- The Holy Spirit *does* move to bring confirmation and faith.
- Mary miracles *do* occur, though they don't always come as babies.

Don and Raissa's experience is a kind of prophecy for all of us, in its own way. It "speaks"—it says the same things the Bible says, and so it is believable. And the whole of this small book has been written to urge you to believe, too.

You and I face a cultural hazard in having so much information, study resources, sermons, tapes and books available today. In some areas, we are inundated with so many of these valuable resources that something mistaken has been concluded. And although other parts of the world may not have such an abundance of materials available, this mistaken philosophy is just as present. Many believe: *To study is to know.*

- People think that way about information.
- Christians think that way about truth.
- You and I might think that way about the Bible.

But it isn't so.

To study the Bible, to be taught the truth or to read a book—including this one—may be a valuable exercise in expanding your base of spiritual information. But *studying* and *knowing* are two different things. The first is an informational pursuit, the second must be incarnational. The first deals with facts as a commodity, the second with life in its intimacy.

"Now Adam knew Eve his wife."[1]

That's the simple way the Bible reports the experience two people had that resulted in the birth of this planet's first child. The word "know" is used in that way, not as a euphemism because God might be too embarrassed to use a more direct term, but because in both Hebrew *(yada')* and Greek *(oida)*, "to know" has always meant more than merely to gain and retain information.

Up Close and Personal

This particular use of the verb "to know" refers to an intimate, intricate, incarnational involvement: to getting "up close and personal," and to life taking flesh through love's dynamic being expressed. So it is that God called you and me *to know:*

- To "know" God's promises and believe them because we are intimate with the

Giver whom we *trust* as faithful;

- To "know" God's Spirit and receive His fullest, deepest workings because we *want* Him as Life-Giver;
- To "know" God's Son and to conceive His newness and expanding purpose within because we *love* Him as Master.

Mary miracles are available everywhere today. I have run the risk of saying so, even though a few theologians often force labored definitions of the miraculous that seem to put God in the position of seeming grudging to grant them, doling miracles only sparingly, and even then, with reluctance.

But I've proposed a hope that I believe is God's intent; a hope I trust this message will help inspire. I've proposed "expecting miracles" with this definition in mind: A miracle is *any invasion of earth with the workings and grace of heaven's power, love and life.* And I believe God's promises reveal that an abundance of these miracles are waiting in the wings, some of them perhaps being announced through this small book as the Holy Spirit may use it to speak. Perhaps to you. Perhaps now.

I am inviting you to hear Him speak, and to welcome the certainty of God's love for you. And I'm urging you to "become expectant" with confidence in His promises as you fully allow His

Spirit to move upon you. Now.

There's a promise He's whispering to you.

There's a dream He's giving you, and you can't escape the feeling, "It's really *God* telling me this!"

So receive it. Don't be afraid, for God is able to bring into being anything necessary to fulfill His Word, and He fully desires to increase His joy and fruitfulness in *your* life. So open wide with faith, and prepare to move forward in joy.

Someone is on the phone.

For you.

❧

Questions for Reflection

Chapter 1
1. Do you see the parallel between Mary's miracle conception and God's readiness to bring His Word of promise to pass in you?
2. Can you remember a time when you were faced with the possibility of God "impregnating" you with a promise in His Word?
3. How did that event change your life?
4. Does an area of your life need a "Mary miracle" today?
5. Are you open to asking God for that miracle?

6. What factors might hold someone back from doing so?

Chapter 2

1. Do you ever sense you've heard God's "voice," or is hearing from God an unfamiliar concept to you?
2. Have you had times when you were unsure whether the voice you were hearing was God's, your own or possibly that of a deceiving spirit?
3. What are some steps you can take to help you determine whose voice it is you are hearing? Can you think of biblical instances of God speaking to people? How many?
4. Have there been times you've dismissed what could have been God's voice as just your imagination simply because the time or setting seemed inappropriate?
5. Is it possible you've missed God's voice on occasion because you deemed yourself unworthy of hearing from Him?

Chapter 3

1. What does the statement "There are no miracles without the Mary miracle" mean to you?

2. Why is the "Mary miracle" the "fountain-head miracle"?
3. When God began the Mary miracle in your life, what do you believe was His ultimate purpose?
4. How does it change your life to know that you, like Mary, have been "chosen" by God?
5. What does the "continuing wonder" of God's redemptive purposes mean in your life?

Chapter 4

1. How does picturing Mary more as an ordinary young woman affect your thinking?
2. Why do you think the "ordinariness" of Mary's conception has been such a stumbling block to so many?
3. Why do you suppose God didn't choose a more elegant setting for His Son's birth?
4. Are there areas of your life where you feel limited by "ordinariness" as helpless or unpromising as Mary's was?
5. Although a virgin, Mary's womb was tainted with the sin of the Adamic race; yet God spoke life and promise into that womb. Does that affect your perception of the areas of your life where you wrestle with sin?

Chapter 5

1. Mary is referred to as a "highly favored one." How is this also true of you?
2. What does Mary's amazed response to the angel's announcement teach us about our own response to God's messages to us?
3. When are times you have been amazed by God's workings in your life?
4. How did these times increase your understanding and appreciation of grace?
5. How can you more fully be open to God's workings of grace in your life today?

Chapter 6

1. If innocence — or virginity — was an issue in Mary's life, how does this affect our ability to receive the Mary miracle in our own lives?
2. What religious traditions have clouded your perceptions of Mary in the past, preventing you from relating to her as a "real person"?
3. Where has condemnation from past sins and failures blocked your ability to allow God's miracle-workings in your life?
4. By focusing on God's promises and His power, rather than your own human limitations, how does this change your outlook

on your current circumstances?

Chapter 7

1. Do you have a particular area of sin or temptation in your life with which you have struggled for a long period of time, only to despair of ever finding victory?
2. How has this struggle and despair hindered your Christian walk?
3. When you try to accept the fact that God considers you a saint, do you have a hard time doing so?
4. Have you ever considered the possibility that you are dealing with a point of bondage because of past (although forgiven) sins?
5. How can the principle in James 5:16 help set you free from this point of bondage?

Chapter 8

1. What "surprise babies" has God birthed into your life?
2. How were you changed as a result?
3. How were others affected by these "births"?
4. Can you think of any angelic "announcements" that heralded the coming of these births?

5. How can you better cultivate your ability to "listen to the angels" so you will not miss their next announcement to you?

Chapter 9

1. What times in your life have you experienced angelic announcements of impending births, only to look at yourself and your own limitations, and ask, "How can this be?"

2. How did your perspective on the situation change as you began to change your focus from yourself to God?

3. What situations and circumstances did God use to help you change your focus from self to Him?

4. What response do you sense in yourself as you review the list of Bible characters whose experience of breakthrough involved them emotionally?

Chapter 10

1. Consider the amount of stretching God has had to do to bring your faith to the point of conceiving. How much more do you suppose He will have to stretch you to bring that "baby" to full-term delivery?

2. Are you willing to endure the possible dis-

comfort and inconvenience of God's Mary-miracle pregnancy in your life? If not, what is holding you back?

3. Is there something you can do to help you move beyond your reluctance and into a place of excited expectancy?

4. Can you identify times when recklessness has ruined or aborted a Mary miracle in progress in your life?

Chapter 11

1. Can you relate through personal experience to Mary's possible wondering and doubting, once the angel was gone?

2. What signs, if any, can you remember early in your Mary miracle pregnancies that were really "no signs at all"?

3. How did you combat those "no signs at all" that threatened to drag you into unbelief and despair?

4. Have you ever crossed the line between being tempted to doubt and giving in to that doubt to the point that a Mary miracle "kind" of work within you was aborted?

5. How can you better withstand or resist the temptation to give in to doubt during future Mary miracle type "pregnancies"?

Chapter 12

1. What are some of the delays and liabilities you have experienced during times of awaiting God's promises coming to fulfillment in your circumstances?

2. In addition to the new possibilities open to you as a recipient of God's promises, did you accept any new responsibilities or opportunities for service?

3. In what ways have you found occasion to serve someone else's miracle while awaiting the delivery of your own Mary miracle?

4. Can you think of times when singing to, or about, the Lord have strengthened you? What have you seen in this chapter that has accelerated your will to sing?

5. Summarize those applications you might make in your own life, seeing Mary's non-self-defending, non-self-verifying responses.

Chapter 13

1. In what areas of your life might you have experienced a kind of "infertility," preventing you from conceiving God's promises unto fruitfulness?

2. Are there times in your life when God's reassurances, given to you through other people, have run up against your doubts

that say, "This promise couldn't possibly be for me"?

3. Can you think of times in your life when you have received a timely "phone call" from God, only to dismiss it as a "mistake" or a "coincidence"?

4. What are some of the "divine appointments" you have experienced that have changed your life?

5. Have you had times in your life when you have passed from "studying" God's promises to truly "knowing" them on a personal, intimate level?

Notes

Chapter 1
1. See Acts 10:34.
2. Colossians 1:27, italics added.
3. John 3:16.

Chapter 2
1. See Joshua 1:6-9.
2. See 1 John 4:18.

Chapter 3
1. Ephesians 1:4.
2. "Hark! the Herald Angels Sing," written by Charles Wesley (1707-1788), public domain.

Chapter 4

1. See John 1:46.

Chapter 5

1. John 2:5.
2. The phrase "Blessed are you among women" (Luke 1:28) is found in many ancient Greek texts but not in all. Therefore, some readers may not find this phrase in their English translation of the New Testament.
3. See Luke 1:44.
4. See Luke 1:43.
5. See Luke 1:50.

Chapter 7

1. Also see Romans 1:7; 2 Corinthians 1:1; Ephesians 1:1; Philippians 1:1.
2. See 1 Corinthians 6:9-11, italics added.

Chapter 8

1. See Luke 2:11.

Chapter 9

1. Luke 1:38.
2. See Luke 11:11-13.

Chapter 12
1. See Luke 1:7.

Chapter 13
1. Genesis 4:1.